KEEPING OUR
CHEMICAL FACILITIES
SAFE

**A Guide For Implementing DHS' Chemical Facility
Security Vulnerability Assessment Regulations**

Stephen R. Melvin, PE CSP CPP
William R. Benson

We Make the World Safer

PO Box 6873, Alexandria, VA, 22306

NOTICE TO THE READER

Neither the publisher, nor the authors warrant the information provided herein as applicable to every scenario. Both the publisher and the authors expressly disclaim any obligation to provide information other than what has been provided. The authors have taken care to verify the accuracy of the information contained within this book, but refuse to assume responsibility for information which was not available or which may have been provided inaccurately.

The reader is expressly warned that the information provided in this book is provided as a starting point, and that the reader will need to supplement the information provided herein, with information from their own local communities, and with updated information from appropriate sources as the fields of security and safety are dependent on location and adversaries are constantly looking for ways to overcome the latest in security measures.

Neither the publisher, nor the author makes any representation or warranties of any kind, including but not limited to, the warranties of fitness for particular purpose or merchantability, nor are any such representations implied with respect to the material set forth herein. Neither the publisher, nor the author takes any responsibility with respect to such material. Neither the publisher, nor the author shall be liable for any special, consequential, or exemplary damages resulting, in whole or part, from the readers' use of, or reliance upon, this material.

For more information, contact: SRM Associates
                                   PO Box 6873
                                   Alexandria, VA 22306

Library of Congress Control Number: 2009904420
Melvin, Stephen R. Keeping Our Chemical Facilities Safe / Stephen R. Melvin and William R. Benson SRM Associates, August 2007.
ISBN: 1-4392-4006-X. First Hardcopy Edition.

Table of Contents

Appendices

Index of Tables

Foreward

I have been in the business of safety, security, anti-terrorism and emergency preparedness for a long time. I have learned that safety and security are things that people are very interested in – right after an incident. Before an incident, the attitude usually conforms more to the "It hasn't happened here, so it will never happen here." philosophy. It's very difficult to sell "accidents that you didn't have." In spite of that, we here at SRM Associates believe that an ounce of prevention is really worth a pound of cure and our goal is to make the world safer. Put those two things together and you've got an interesting combination. To stretch the ounce/pound metaphor somewhat, we believe that every dollar spent (wisely) on prevention will save sixteen on response and recovery – plus lives.

What that means to us is that we have an obligation to help our clients save money and lives by making effective prevention and preparedness decisions ahead of time rather than just waiting until they are required to put together a plan, and when they are up against a deadline, doing a poor job. We have an obligation to let people know what is coming so that they can effectively plan. And we have an obligation to make the world a better place. We wrote Keeping Our Neighborhoods Safe in order to help families prepare for, respond to, and recover from an attack or a disaster. Since it was published, it has sold well over 2000 copies, and been purchased by government agencies, local governments and business – all to help make the people for whom they were responsible safer. We have written this book for you to make your jobs easier.

If you have a chemical facility and have to comply with these regulations, then this book will take you from the first step of gathering your data, through the process of submitting your information to the Department of Homeland Security, performing your vulnerability assessment, and developing your security plan. If you are a local or state regulator, then the guidance in this document will hopefully allow you to help support your facilities in complying with these regulations. You know they'll be calling you for help. If you work for the Department of Homeland Security, I hope that this book gives you some insight into the businesses that you are regulating and how they will try to meet your regulations. They'll need a lot of help. This is a new program to them. Remember that most of them want to be safe, they want to comply and they are relying on you to provide good guidance to them on what they will need to do, what threats they will need to protect against, and how they can make their plants safer and more secure. At the same time, they have to make chemicals and turn a profit. They don't have the dollars that the federal government (read DOD and DOE) spend to protect facilities, so you will need to work with them closely to help them come up with reasonable, implementable, recommendations.

To all of our readers: thank you for taking the time to read this book. Feedback is always appreciated. Thank you for helping us to make this country safer. We're all in this fight together, and together, we can minimize the threat. Good luck and if you need help, call us.

-Stephen

Chapter

1

Introduction and History – How We Got Here

Why This Book?

After the methyl-isocyanate incident at Bhopal, India in the 1980's, the United States started developing two regulations that changed how the chemical industry did business. The first was the US Occupational Safety and Health Administration's (OSHA) Process Safety Management Regulations (PSM) (29 CFR 1910) and the second was the Environmental Protection Agency's (EPA) Risk Management Program Regulations (RMP) (40 CFR 112(r)).

In 1990, the EPA was tasked by Congress to regulate and enforce the Clean Air Act Amendments. These amendments require all facilities using certain amounts of hazardous chemicals to develop accident and release prevention strategies for their facilities.

In 1992, OSHA released their PSM standards including a list of covered chemicals and their threshold quantities (TQ[1]). The

---

1 A Threshold Quantity list provides the amounts of hazardous chemicals

regulations required covered facilities to implement programs to manage changes to processes and chemicals, ensure that the data on the plant was up to date, review each part of the process for potentially dangerous steps, actions, procedures, and more.

The Risk Management Program Rule was written to implement Section 112(r) of the Clean Air Act amendments. By June 21, 1999, every chemical facility subject to these amendments was required to submit a summary of its Risk Management Program (RMP) to the EPA, revising and resubmitting it every five years. By complying with these requirements, chemical facilities have gained a great degree of familiarity with conducting risk assessment studies to prevent accidental releases of hazardous chemicals. Then, in 2001, the United States was attacked on its own soil by Islamist Terrorists.

Five years later, Congress passed the 2006 Homeland Security Appropriations Act which required the Department of Homeland Security (DHS) to develop regulations for implementing Chemical Facility Anti-Terrorism (CSAT) standards. Most of the facilities that are currently required to submit RMPs and/or develop PSM programs must also comply with this new regulation. As with the safety programs, the new regulations will require a risk assessment study, but the emphasis will be on security vulnerabilities rather than vulnerabilities to accidental releases.

Safety Managers of chemical facilities, while mindful of the requirements of the PSM program and RMP Rule, may not be familiar with the security specific aspects of the CSAT. This book will provide clarification and explanation of these security aspects, and also seeks to provide guidance to facilities that are not required to comply with either PSM or RMP regulations, so that they can develop a Security Vulnerability Assessment (SVA) from the ground up, and can avoid many of the pitfalls inherent in tackling such a difficult project.

It is because of this change in focus that this book was written.

---

over which a facility is required to comply with the regulations.

In addition to the new focus on security, the CSAT also contained a new list of "chemicals of interest", which if present at a facility, may make that facility subject to the CSAT' Security Vulnerability Assessment (SVA) process. This list is similar to the TQ lists from both the PSM program and the RMP Rule. This new list (published as Appendix A of the new regulations) contains many of the same chemicals as those listed on the RMP and PSM TQ lists, but they may have different thresholds. Additionally, there are chemicals on the list that are not listed on either of the RMP or PSM lists, which means that many facilities that were not subject to the old safety regulations may be subject to the new security regulations.

This book will discuss the new CSAT regulations, how the CSAT came to be in their present form, and the preparation, conduct, and interpretation of results of a Security Vulnerability Study.

The Regulations

The basis of the new CSAT requirements can be found in the following text, taken from the Federal Register 6 CFR Part 27: Chemical Facility Anti-Terrorism Standards; Final Rule.

> *"On October 4, 2006, the President signed the Department of Homeland Security Appropriations Act of 2007 (the Act), which provides the Department of Homeland Security with the authority to regulate the security of high-risk chemical facilities. See Pub. L. 109-295, sec. 550.*
>
> *Section 550 requires the Secretary of Homeland Security to promulgate interim final regulations ``establishing risk-based performance standards for security of chemical facilities" by April 4, 2007. Although interim final regulations are usually issued without prior*

notice and comment (and the Act requires neither), the Department issued an Advance Notice of Rulemaking (Advance Notice) seeking comment on the significant issues and regulatory text.

As discussed more fully in the Advance Notice, before the enactment of Section 550, the Federal government did not have authority to regulate the security of most chemical facilities. The Department has, however, worked closely with industry leaders in pursuit of voluntary enhancement of security at these facilities and provided both technical assistance and grant funding for security. In addition, through the Coast Guard's Maritime Security regulations, the Department has addressed security at certain maritime-related chemical facilities.

Recently, the Departments of Homeland Security and Transportation also proposed security regulations for the rail transportation of hazardous chemicals. Other Federal programs have addressed chemical facility safety, but not security: the Environmental Protection Agency (EPA) regulates chemical process safety through its Risk Management Plan (RMP) program; the Department of Labor's Occupational Safety and Health Administration (OSHA) regulates workplace safety and health at chemical facilities; the Department of Commerce oversees compliance with the Chemical Weapons Convention; and the Department of Justice's Bureau of Alcohol, Tobacco, Firearms, and Explosives (ATF) regulates, through licenses and permits, the purchase, possession, storage, and transportation of explosives.

With the authority under Section 550, the Department can now fill a significant security gap in the country's anti-terrorism efforts. Section 550 specifies that the regulations ``shall apply to chemical facilities that, in the discretion of the Secretary, present high levels of security risk."

The statute requires that the regulations establish

risk-based performance standards; requires Security Vulnerability Assessments and Site Security Plans; allows Alternative Security Programs; mandates audits and inspections to determine compliance with the regulations; provides for civil penalties for violation of an order issued under the statute; and allows the Secretary to order a facility to cease operations if the facility is not in compliance with the requirements. The statute also gives the Department the authority to protect from inappropriate public disclosure any information developed pursuant to Section 550, ``including vulnerability assessments, site security plans, and other security related information, records, and documents.''"[2]

History Of The Regulations

Following the terrorist attacks of 11 September, 2001, the Department of Homeland Security (DHS) began to evaluate the need for an increased level of security pertaining to the storage of hazardous chemicals in facilities within the United States. Though many chemical facilities instituted voluntary security measures, DHS determined that voluntary measure alone were insufficient to ensure the security of the Nation. DHS sought *"and achieved the authority to establish and require imple-mentation of risk-based per-formance standards for the security of our Nations' high-rick chemical facilities..." (6 CFR Part 27)*

Existing regulations required facilities that processed, used,

2 Chemical Facility Anti-Terrorism Standards; Final Rule.

or stored chemicals that were of a given type and were over a given threshold quantity, to perform analyses of their affected facilities. These analyses not only gave the facility's management an overall picture of exposure the the risk of accidental releases, but also provided various regulatory agencies with proof of compliance with the regulations.

Before September 11, 2001, the main emphasis of these requirements was to decrease the risk of an accidental release of hazardous chemicals to facility workers, surrounding communities, and the environment. They primarily examined process units and storage facilities for sound operating procedures and proper safeguards designed to reduce accidental/mechanical failures. Very little emphasis was placed on security issues that might place the facility at risk of a terrorist attack becaause people just didn't believe that it would happen. In many instances, security related issues were given a cursory examination, primarily concerned with internal and perimeter security measures. At that time, the idea that a chemical storage facility or refinery might be a terrorist target was given little credibility. After the 9/11 attacks, this perspective underwent a radical change. Terrorists had demonstrated their willingness and capability to inflict damage on American interests. In 2003, DHS began the process of developing a standardized way to regulate the security of these facilities against possible terrorist actions. On December 28, 2006, DHS released draft regulations to implement Section 550 of the Homeland Security Appropriations Act of 2007.

These regulations underwent a comment period, and DHS revised them to release final regulations on April 9, 2007. The final regulations incorporated many of the changes requested by those who commented, but did not address any changes to the methodology (called RAMCAP) included in the draft regulations. Therefore, the Chemical Security and Anti-Terrorism (CSAT) methodology described in this book will be based upon the methodology from the draft regulations.

Chapter

2

Requirements Overview – The Big Picture

What Must A Facility Do To Comply?

There are three requirements in the methodology proposed by DHS. The first step of the methodology is a data gathering process called the CSAT Top–Screen. In a nutshell, the Top–Screen process is the process by which DHS will evaluate the information provided by facilities to determine how much of a risk they pose, and to classify them into tiers which will determine what standards they must follow. The second step of the methodology requires the facility to conduct a Security Vulnerability Assessment. The facility will evaluate the possible attacks that might occur, determine if there are adequate measures in place to deter, detect, delay, and respond to an adversary, and recommend possible additional measures that could help prevent an attack from an adversary. The third step in the methodology is to develop a Site Security Plan (SSP), by which the facility will implement the recommendations that were determined during the SVA. The SSP must contain seventeen specific items called out in the regulations to include, plans for addressing the threats stipulated by DHS, securing the

perimeter, protecting computer assets, and more. At the time of this writing, the Top–Screen process will be conducted via a secure website provided by DHS[3]. DHS believes that entering the Top-Screen data will take a facility approximately 30 hrs.

Who Must Comply?

Any facility that has over the threshold quantity of a chemical listed in Appendix A (of the regulations and this book) must submit their information through the Top-Screen process to DHS. The quantity of a chemical is defined as the amount of the chemical expected to present within a radius of 170 feet at any given time. Once the information is received, DHS will inform the facility as to which tier requirements the facility will need to adopt.

Mixtures

As of this writing, DHS has not provided any guidance on how mixtures will be handled in determining whether a quantity of the mixture exceeds the threshold quantity. A conservative approach is for the facility to assume that if the chemical is in a mixture greater than 1% by weight, the entire quantity of the mixture should be counted toward the threshold quantity. While this seems exorbitant, there are some regulations that do determine quantities of chemicals through this method. A less conservative approach would be to treat the mixtures as the RMP regulation treats them, which is to count only the weight that is within the mixture

---

3   http://www.dhs.gov/xprevprot/programs/gc_1169501486197.shtm

toward the quantity. For example, if a facility has 5,000 lbs of a 50% solution of Ammonium Hydroxide, then the facility only has 2,500 lbs of ammonia. Whatever method your facility chooses, the company needs to be able to provide a reasonable justification of the methodology until DHS provides guidance on this calculation.

Facility Exemptions[4]

- **Facilities regulated pursuant to the Maritime Transportation Safety Act (MTSA)**. The Department will apply the MTSA exemption to facilities regulated under 33 CFR Part 105, Maritime Facility Security regulations. Part 105 of Title 33 of the Code of Federal Regulations is the only regulation that imposes the security plan requirements of 46 U.S.C. 70103 on maritime facilities. If the facility site includes both a facility regulated pursuant to the Maritime Transportation Security Act of 2002, Public Law 107-295, as amended, and a facility not regulated pursuant to the Maritime Transportation Security Act, the facility shall select "Partially" when filling out the statutory exemption page of the Top-Screen. The facility should then complete the remainder of the Top-Screen for the facility not subject to Maritime Transportation Security Act.

- **Public Water Systems, as defined in the Safe Drinking Water Act**. If a facility contains a unit that is a Public Water System regulated under the Safe Drinking Water Act, but also contains components that are not so regulated, the facility shall select "Partially" when filling out the statutory exemption page of the Top-Screen. The facility should then complete the remainder of the Top-Screen for the portion of the facility that is not exempted (i.e., the portion of the facility that is not regulated under the Safe Drinking Water Act).

---

4   Excerpted from "Identifying Facilities Covered by the Chemical Security Regulation Webpage."

- **Water Treatment Facilities, as defined in the Federal Water Pollution Control Act**. If the facility site contains Treatment Works regulated under the Federal Water Pollution Control Act, but also contains a facility or portion of a facility not so regulated, the facility shall select "Partially" when filling out the statutory exemption page of the Top-Screen. The facility should then complete the remainder of the Top-Screen for the portion of the facility that is not exempted (i.e., the facility or portion of the facility that is not regulated under the Federal Water Pollution Control Act).

- **Facilities owned or operated by the Department of Defense or the Department of Energy.**

- **Facilities subject to regulation by the Nuclear Regulatory Commission (NRC)**. The Department will apply the NRC statutory exemption only to facilities where NRC already imposes significant requirements and regulates the safety and security of most of the facility, not just a few radioactive sources. For example, a power reactor holding a license under 10 CFR Part 50, a special nuclear material fuel cycle holding a license under 10 CFR Part 70, and facilities licensed under 10 CFR Parts 30 and 40 that have received security orders requiring increased protection, are all exempt from 6 CFR Part 27. A facility that only possesses small radioactive sources for chemical process control equipment, gauges, and dials is not exempt.

The CSAT-Top Screen Process

Appendix A of the CSAT regulations lists the threshold quantities of "chemicals of interest" deemed hazardous and worthy of concern. Chemical facilities who have listed chemicals on their site over the TQ will submit their chemical inventories and other information to DHS through a process called the Top–Screen. The Top–Screen is completed through an Internet based interface that

allows facilities to securely[5] input the required data to DHS. The Department of Homeland Security will use the data collected by the Top-Screen input to classify the facility into one of four Tiers[6]. Each Tier is based partially on the degree of risk that the facility faces according the the amount and type of chemicals it contains. Other criteria include the amount of damage that a facility can do to the public if there is a release, the economic impact of losing the revenue to that community, the strategic impact of losing the product that the facility produces, the damage that could be done if a facility's chemicals were removed and used in another location, etc.

The criteria for ranking a facility may change in the future, as DHS gets a handle on the vast amounts of information through which they will need to sort. Tier 1 is assigned to the facilities that have the highest risk ranking, and Tier 4 to the lowest. DHS will use the submitted data to determine whether a facility should be covered under these statutes, whether it presents a high level of security risk, and if so, into which tier the facility should be classified.

At the time of this writing, the exact configuration of the Top Screen is classified, however, the Department of Homeland Security's Chemical Facility Anti-Terrorism Standards Registration Page[7] states that submitters be prepared to submit the following information prior to registering for the CVAS Top-Screen process:

- Name of Facility Street Address

---

5 Note that there is currently no Virtual Private Network or other electronically-based method for ensuring that the information is not intercepted, so the facility is relying on their browser security to ensure the security of their data.
6 The methodology for classifying the facilities into tiers is classified, so we will not be able to guide facilities through the process in a step-by-step fashion. Another drawback is that facilities will not be able to determine based on the Top-Screen process what actions they can take to reduce their risk. This places the facility in the position of being reactive rather than proactive.
7 Accessing the Chemical Security Assessment Tool (CSAT) Webpage.

- City, State, and Zip Code
- Country
- Latitude (in decimal degrees) -- this is a positive number
- Longitude (in decimal degrees) -- this is a negative number and must have a "-" sign prior to the numeric designation

The regulations also indicate that the following information may be required during the initial registration process:

- Whether a toxic release worst-case scenario (as identified by the facility under the EPA Risk Management Program) might expose a residential population greater than or equal to 200,000 persons, and if so, whether the distance in such a scenario might exceed 25 miles.
- Whether a flammable release worst-case scenario (as identified by the facility under the EPA Risk Management Program) might expose a residential population greater than or equal to 1,000 persons.
- Whether the facility manufactures or stores explosive materials in sufficient quantities to result in an off site residential exposed population.
- Whether the facility has any specified chemical weapon or chemical weapon precursors.

To address economic impacts, the tool may ask the facility the following types of questions:

- Whether the facility produces products of national economic importance or whose loss could negatively impact multiple economic sectors.
- Whether an attack on the facility could cause collateral physical damage to key transportation assets.

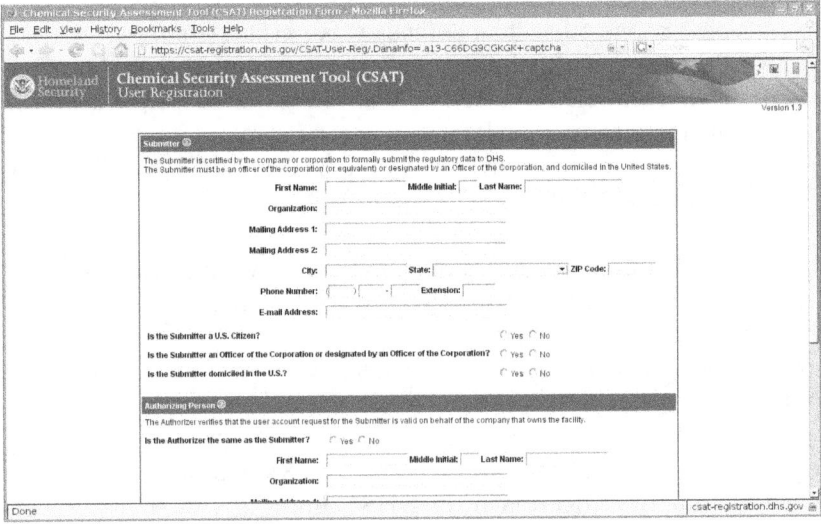

CSAT Screenshot

To address mission impacts the tool may ask questions, such as whether the facility:

- Has chemical(s) for which it provides 35% of the U.S. domestic production capacity.
- Is the sole U.S. supplier.
- Produces a chemical or product used in the manufacture of defense weapons.
- Produces a chemical or product supplied to and for use by multiple defense weapons systems contractors.

- Is a major chemical supplier (>35% market share) to DOD for reasons other than defense weapons systems.
- Produces a chemical or product directly to another manufacturer, producer, or distributor for subsequent use in the manufacture of defense weapons systems.
- Serves as a major or sole supplier to a public health, water treatment, or power generation facility.

A booklet of questions that DHS has developed to assist facilities in filling out the Top-Screen website can be downloaded from this website: http://www.dhs.gov/xlibrary/assets/chemsec_csattopscreenquestions .pdf.

Facilities that are determined to be high-risk under this regulation will be required to complete the SVA process once they receive written notification from DHS. Initial CSAT Top-Screens are due within 60 calendar days of the date that "Appendix A: DHS Chemicals of Interest" is published in the Federal Register as final, or within 60 calendar days of coming into possession of any such Chemical of Interest at or above the Threshold Quantities. As of the time of this writing, Appendix A has not been finalized.

> **If a facility fails to submit a Top–Screen inventory DHS will presumptively classify that facility as "High-Risk" regardless of the amount of chemicals or explosives stored at the facility, and the facility will automatically be required to continue the SVA process.**

The Chemical Facility Assessment Tool

Once a facility is notified by DHS, they will be required to complete a Chemical Facility Vulnerability Assessment within 90 days. At the time of this writing, the only approved method for conducting this assessment is the Chemical Facility Assessment Tool (CFAT). The CFAT is based upon the RAMCAP

methodology, which is a tool developed by a working group from the American Society of Mechanical Engineers (the ASME Innovative Technologies Institute) together with subject matter experts. DHS worked together with this institute to develop a methodology that would allow it to identify chemical facilities most at risk to terrorist attack, and assist those facilities in reducing that risk, or mitigating the effects of terrorist attacks against those facilities. On December 28, 2006, combining the "best practices" of these entities, DHS released the CFAT.

The RAMCAP executive summary states:

> RAMCAP™ (Risk Analysis and Management for Critical Asset Protection) is a framework for analyzing and managing the risks associated with terrorist attacks against critical infrastructure assets. RAMCAP™ provides a consistent and technically sound methodology to identify, analyze, quantify and communicate the various characteristics and impacts that may lead terrorists to select a particular target, and the impacts from a specific form of attack. It documents a process for identifying security vulnerabilities and provides methods to evaluate the options for improving these weaknesses.[8]

To create the CFAT, DHS drew upon existing regulations set forth by other Federal Agencies for guidance in the area of chemical facility risk management.

---

8 RAMCAP™. p1.

Contributing Agency	Applicable Regulations
Environmental Protection Agency (EPA)	Risk Management Program (RMP)
Occupational Safety and Health Administration (OSHA)	Various
Department of Commerce (DOC)	Chemical Weapons Convention oversight
Department of Justice Bureau of Alcohol, Tobacco, and Firearms (DOJ-ATF)	Various

Table 1: Federal Agencies contributions to DHS's Chemical Facility Vulnerability Assessment Tool

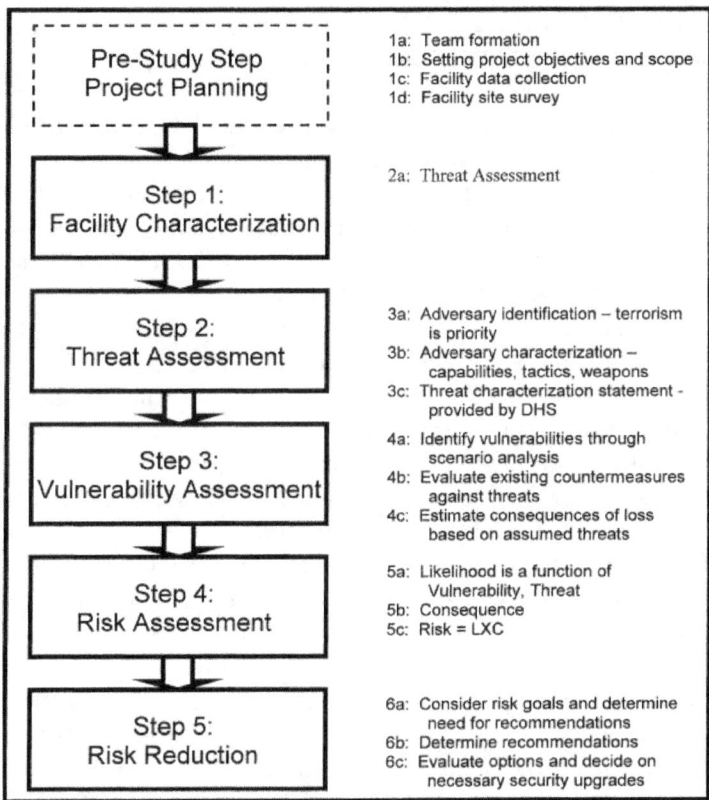

The 5 Step CFAT Process.

The Chemical Facility Assessment Tool is a team-based, multi-step step process that examines how a covered facility addresses specific types of terrorist threats. The process is shown in Figure 1.

DHS also recognized the expertise of the private chemical refining industry, and attempted to achieve its goals within the chemical industry's existing history of compliance to federal guidelines and regulations. The current cycles for updates however, have the facilities introducing a completely new cycle into the

rotations that they are currently managing. For example, a Tier 1 facility that is also a Program Level 3 RMP facility and is subject to PSM will have the following updates:

- Every three years, they must audit their RMP program and ensure that it is being followed adequately
- Every five years, they must update their Process Hazard Analyses (PHA) and their Risk Management Plans
- Every year, they need to review and evaluate their Emergency Response Plans for accuracy and currency
- Every two years, they must update their Vulnerability Assessment and Site Security Plan.

Additionally, there is the problem of Community Right To Know (CRTK) information. The purpose behind PSM is to protect employees and so they need to have access to the information that is developed to support the PSM program. The purpose of RMP is to protect the public from releases of dangerous chemicals, and part of that program is the right of the local community to know what is in their backyard. The CSAT regulation muddies the waters. By making the information developed during this program security sensitive information, a facility may have difficulty determining which information is developed in support of this program, and which information is developed in support of other programs that allow release of the information. An example would be the quantity of a chemical kept on site. While it is security sensitive information, it is also Community Right To Know information under the Risk Management Program regulations. In other words, it will cost the average facility some time in determining what information should be released and what shouldn't.

What is Chemical Vulnerability Information (CVI) and What is Community Right To Know (CRTK)?

The Site Security Plan

Once a facility is notified by DHS, they will be required to complete a Site Security Plan within 120 days of the notification. That means that no later than 30 days after they have to submit an SVA, they have to submit their plan for fixing the holes. It also means that DHS will most likely have not had a chance to review the SVA before the facility will need to send in their plan for

securing the site. An SSP will require that the facility address each of the vulnerabilities determined during their SVA, in addition to 17 elements specifically called out in the regulations by DHS.

Updates

Tier 1 and Tier 2 facilities will need to update their SVAs and SSPs every two years. Tier 3 and Tier 4 facilities will need to update their SVAs and SSPs every three years.

Requirement	Due Date
Top Screen	60 days after publication of Appendix A in the Federal Register
Security Vulnerability Assessment (SVA)	90 days after notification from DHS that the facility needs to complete an SVA and SSP.
Site Security Plan (SSP)	120 days after notification from DHS that the facility needs to complete an SVA and SSP.
Tier 1 and 2 updates	Every 2 years after initial submission **OR** Upon a change to the SVA/SSP
Tier 3 and 4 updates	Every 3 years after initial submission **OR** Upon a change to the SVA/SSP

Table 2: Calendar of Due Dates for Compliance with DHS regulations

Chapter

3

The Vulnerability Assessment

Preparing For The Study

The Vulnerability Assessment Study Team

The Vulnerability Assessment Core Team is the cornerstone of the Vulnerability Assessment Process. It should include full-time members who are intimately knowledgeable in their duties and responsibilities. Like any project, if you have members on the team who are not the best representatives from the company, then you will not end up with the best study. We have seen safety studies where the company put members on the team who should not have been there, because the company didn't want to pull their best employees off the line. Their study was not as good as others. There is a programming term called GIGO, which means: "Garbage In, Garbage Out." The same is true here; put your best people on the team, and you'll get the best study.

> If you don't have time to do it right, when will you have time to do it over? – John Wooden

Since it may cost a significant amount to have to redo portions of the study if DHS finds it to be insufficient, by doing the best job possible up front, the company is likely to save money in the long run.

Scoping the Study

Before holding any team sessions, the Team Leader/Facilitator should hold a pre-meeting with facility management to discuss and finalize the following items:

- Scope of the Study – while it is obvious where the perimeter of the plant is, the study will need to address whether the facility is going to work together with neighbors (for the SVA), what level of detail will be needed by the team, how the team will work together with management, the elements that will be covered, how the team will prioritize facilities (in the event of multiple locations), etc.
- Expected Schedule – when will the team visit the site, when can they expect to meet for team meetings, when will subject matter experts be needed (e.g. utilities, or support services), etc.
- Study Participants – who will make up the core team, who will serve as subject matter experts, and will there be any participation from other agencies or businesses. Note that the core team must include a representative from operations, a person who understands the engineering of the system, and a security representative at the facility. The core team must also include a Team Leader/Facilitator who is familiar with the process of conducting a Vulnerability Assessment.
- Risk Ranking Matrix – DHS provided a Risk Ranking Matrix in the original proposed regulations, but the regulations do not require that the facility use that matrix. The matrix provided does not match up with matrices traditionally used by chemical facilities in meeting safety requirements, and it falls to management to understand the difference between the risks or to decide to use their

existing matrices for consistency. Risk Matrices include values assigned for likelihood and severity, and requirements to mitigate a higher risk to an acceptable risk. It is vital that management understand the consequences of choosing a particular risk matrix as a poor choice will either result in a study that has no useful recommendations or will require the company to commit resources correcting vulnerabilities that are not truly high risk.

> **It is vital that management understand the consequences of choosing a particular risk matrix.**

A team can easily become overwhelmed by the scope of the project, so most teams will break the facility into manageable sections (sometimes called "nodes") that will allow the Study Team to focus on a portion of the facility at a time. (The way to eat an elephant is "one bite at a time.") For example, the team may decide to analyze the facility by geographic areas (tank farm, specific units, etc.) or may break them down by assets. The following list describes a few ways to break down the facility into manageable portions:

- By equipment (and associated piping)
- By geographic location
- By security zones
- By responsible individuals (i.e. different units may need different operators, engineers, etc.)
- By chemicals
- By process

The team leader should determine the best way to break the facility down to keep the study team focused and able to complete the study in the shortest possible time. Choosing a facilitator who can move the team quickly can save the company a significant amount of money by allowing each team member to return to their regular duties as quickly as possible. For the same reason, the other team members should be some of the best that the facility has. Just a few of the hidden costs of prolonging a study by having a poor

facilitator or other team members include:
- Salaries/Benefits
- Loss of production
- Overtime
- Facility rental costs
- Drinks/Snacks/Meals (if they are provided by the company)
- Power Consumption

By applying a rigorous analysis to each section of the facility, the team will be able to focus on that section while knowing that the rest of the facility will be addressed in other sections of the study later. One example of this type of sectioning is the "nodes" from a Hazard and Operability Study (HAZOP).

The general rule for focusing on a given node is that causes can only be contained within the node, but consequences can happen anywhere. By performing an entire study using the premises of this rule, the team can be assured that any cause within the entire facility has been addressed. Although the team leader typically pre-assigns these sections, they should be agreed upon by all Team Members.

Members of the Team and Qualifications

The team will be broken apart into two different groups: full-time core members and part-time subject matter experts. The first group will include the positions required by the regulations and any additional team members that management wants to assign to the team for the duration of the study. The second group will include any subject matter experts that the team will need to consult to answer various questions as they come up during the study. A good team can use this second group effectively by calling them in only when needed and by collecting several questions to present to the experts at a single time. If the team needs to call in a subject matter expert numerous times in order to progress, they should consider adding that expert to the team as a regular member.

Full-time members of the team (* indicates member is required by the regulations) should include:
- ***The Team Leader*** (or Facilitator) – The Team Leader will

drive the effectiveness of the Team. He/she should have experience leading team-based studies. By law, the Team Leader must be completely knowledgeable of the Vulnerability Assessment Methodology. The Team Leader is responsible for scheduling the study sessions and arranging for the actual meeting place of the Team. He/she is responsible for coordinating any pre-study documentation (Piping & Instrumentation Diagrams, Process Flow Diagrams, etc.), any audio-visual or records-keeping technology or documentation needs. The Team Leader will ultimately be responsible for generating the final report and delivering it to the facility management. He/she may be assisted in documentation of the study by a *scribe* who will document the study, assist in development of the final report, and coordinate records necessary for the completion of the study. Typically, the scribe tracks study progress and helps the facilitator ensure that none of the information is missing prior to completion of the final report.

- * ***Operations representative*** – The Operations representative will provide the team with knowledge of the facility's process and equipment operations. Usually this person is one of the senior operators. This person has the experience to know what will happen if an adversary tries various attacks. They can also help the team to understand the operational impact of the recommendations that the team develops. For example, if the team were to recommend requiring an extensive background check on all employees, then the Operations representative should be able to explain the pitfalls that the union might introduce to implementing that recommendation. Similarly, if the team were to recommend an increased number of gates with keys between the areas of the plant, the Operations representative should be able to explain the impact on process operations of creating all of those extra steps.
- * ***Engineering representative*** – This individual understands the engineering behind the process. With good engineering

judgment, they can help determine what the consequences of an adversary's attack will be, and will help to provide a balanced understanding of any recommendations that affect the process itself. For example, the Engineering representative should be able to explain the economic impact on the company of a recommendation to change a process chemical to a less hazardous one.

- ** Security representative* – The security representative should have knowledge and experience of the facility's security procedures, methods, equipment, and systems. This person should understand how the security procedures interact with the equipment and should have a good knowledge of the impacts to changing either equipment or procedures. It is not necessary, but can be very helpful if the Security Representative knows how much the implementation measures will cost. If the Security Representative does not know this information, then the team will need to acquire that information before a final cost-benefit analysis can be done as the last part of the study.

- *Safety representative* – While not required by the regulations, the Safety representative should have knowledge of the facility's process hazards, process safety procedures, methods, and systems, and should be able to help the facility understand any impacts that recommendations would have on existing safety programs.

- *Facility representative* – The Facility representative will provide information regarding the facility's design, including asset value, function, criticality, and procedures.

- *Informations Systems/Automation representative* – The Information Systems/Automation representative will provide information on the information systems technologies and cyber security provisions, as well as knowledge of the facility's process control systems. It is possible that this person be brought in as a part-time team member, but for facilities that are completely automated,

this person may be the only one who truly understands the control logic and impacts of the SCADA (Supervisory Control and Data Acquisition) system.

The Core Team may be augmented by part-time Team Members. These members may have specific areas of expertise not normally available in the facility's staff:

- *Security Specialists* – Security Specialists will have in-depth knowledge of threat assessments, terrorism, weapons, targeting and insurgency/guerrilla warfare, or specialized knowledge of detection technologies or other countermeasures available. They may have experience with military or Department of Energy facilities, they may have experience in corporate security or law enforcement and they may even have security certifications such as the American Society for Industrial Security's Certified Protection Professional (CPP) designation. They will often be useful in helping the team understand how various adversaries will carry out their attacks. Their biggest drawback is that they usually have a single view based on their experience that can handicap their understanding of what a private chemical facility can do to prevent incidents. Especially vulnerable to this liability are experts who have worked on Federal Government Projects such as military or Department Of Energy (DOE) facilities as a chemical facility will not have the same level of resources to carry out recommendations as government facilities, therefore they may encourage the team to recommend corrective actions that either the company will not carry out because they are too expensive (thereby opening the company up to possible fines or liability for not completing recommendations in their SVA) or which they may carry out but which will not be cost effective.
- *Cyber Security Specialist* – The Cyber Security Specialist will have knowledge of cyber security practices and technologies. This includes possible attacks, current technologies for defeating those attacks, proper procedures

to prevent computer espionage or to prevent an adversary from gaining control of the SCADA system, wireless technologies, etc.

- ***Process Design Specialist*** – A Process Specialist will bring expertise in the process design to the team. While this specialist is similar to the Engineering representative, this person may have more in-depth information on the design, especially for new units.

- ***Management Representative*** – A representative from Management will bring a knowledge of the facility's business management practices, goals, budgets, plans, economic impacts, and other management systems to the Team. Many teams choose to have information from this person provided separately from the team sessions in order to prevent a feeling that management will "punish those who speak out."

- ***Other Subject Matter Experts*** – Depending on the nature of the facility being studied, there may be a need to add experts in various fields to the Team. These Experts may be knowledgeable about the specific equipment contained in the Process Unit, or they may have in-depth knowledge of the various scientific aspects of the facility, etc.

Documentation Needed for the Study

Before beginning a Security Vulnerability Assessment, the team should have certain information at its disposal. As an example from the Safety field, before beginning a Process Hazard Analysis, it is essential that the team have an up to date Emergency Response Plan, Process Safety Information, and Operating Procedures. Process Safety Information includes such things as Piping and Instrumentation Diagrams (P&IDs), Process Parameters (Pressures, Temperatures, Flows, etc.), Materials of Construction, etc. This information is as useful in developing consequences from deliberate events as it is in developing consequences from accidental events, so it should be present and up to date for the Security Vulnerability

Assessment as well. According to the PSM Regulations, Process Safety Information (29 CFR 1910.119(d)) includes:

Process safety information: In accordance with the schedule set forth in paragraph (e)(1) of this section, the employer shall complete a compilation of written process safety information before conducting any process hazard analysis required by the standard. The compilation of written process safety information is to enable the employer and the employees involved in operating the process to identify and understand the hazards posed by those processes involving highly hazardous chemicals. This process safety information shall include information pertaining to the hazards of the highly hazardous chemicals used or produced by the process, information pertaining to the technology of the process, and information pertaining to the equipment in the process.

Material Safety Data Sheets

    (1) Information pertaining to the hazards of the highly hazardous chemicals in the process. This information shall consist of at least the following:

      (i) Toxicity information;

      (ii) Permissible exposure limits;

(iii) Physical data;

(iv) Reactivity data;

(v) Corrosivity data;

(vi) Thermal and chemical stability data; and

(vii) Hazardous effects of inadvertent mixing of different materials that could foreseeably occur.

(2) **Note:** Material Safety Data Sheets meeting the requirements of 29 CFR 1910.1200(g) may be used to comply with this requirement to the extent they contain the information required by this subparagraph.

(3) Information pertaining to the technology of the process.

(i) Information concerning the technology of the process shall include at least the following:

(A) A block flow diagram or simplified process flow diagram (see Appendix B to this section);

(B) Process chemistry;

(C) Maximum intended inventory;

(D) Safe upper and lower limits for such items as temperatures, pressures,

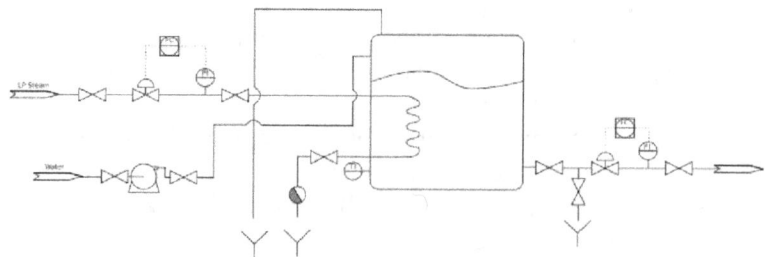

Example Piping and Instrumentation Diagram

flows or compositions; and,

(E) An evaluation of the consequences of deviations, including those affecting the safety and health of employees.

(ii) Where the original technical information no longer exists, such information may be developed in conjunction with the process hazard analysis in sufficient detail to support the analysis.

(4) Information pertaining to the equipment in the process.

(i) Information pertaining to the equipment in the process shall include:

(A) Materials of construction;

(B) Piping and instrument diagrams (P&ID's)[9];

(C) Electrical classification;

(D) Relief system design and design basis;

(E) Ventilation system design;

(F) Design codes and standards employed;

(G) Material and energy balances for processes built after May 26, 1992; and,

(H) Safety systems (e.g. interlocks, detection or suppression systems).

(ii) The employer shall document that equipment complies with recognized and generally accepted good engineering practices.

(iii) For existing equipment designed and constructed in accordance with codes, standards, or practices that are no longer in general use, the employer shall

---

9 http://en.wikipedia.org/wiki/Piping_and_instrumentation_diagram. Accessed 19 August 2007.

determine and document that the equipment is designed, maintained, inspected, tested, and operating in a safe manner.

In addition to this safety information which will help the team to determine the consequences of any attacks, and the possible assets that might be stolen from or damaged at the facility, the team should also consider assembling the following information:

- Facility blueprints, plot plans, equipment layouts and area maps
- Lists of raw materials and products produced
- Existing company standards and security best practices
- Local Emergency Planning Commission response plans
- Product throughput and product parameters

- Historical security incident reviews
- Company personnel interviews

- Site photographs
- Elevation drawings
- Local maps
- Pipeline alignment drawings
- Emergency response procedures
- Police agency response plans
- Support infrastructure reviews

Additional information may be found in historical documentation, product testing and evaluation reports, maintenance records, ME&I reports, and operations manuals. However, the amount of information and working data contained in the mind and memory of an experienced Operator or long-time employee cannot and should not be discounted. The Team Leader must be prepared to draw this data out during the team sessions.

Performing a Vulnerability Assessment is a structured, intensive analysis, where the Study Team examines and analyzes all

aspects of a facility's assets, seeking vulnerabilities that affect the outcome of the entire study by taking into consideration possibilities not previously considered. In this light, comprehensive data gathering is one of the most important aspects of preparing for the Vulnerability Study. The quality of the analysis will only be as good as the data available to the team.

The data required will depend on the facility location, type of processes at the facility, and volume of chemicals onsite. Data will also be required in regards to outside security support, threat types, and other infrastructure issues. DHS separates data into four categories:

- Facility and Right of Way records
- System Informations
- Operations Records
- Outside Support and Regulatory Issues

The Walk-through

At least part of the team must perform a detailed walk-through of the site. Without a walk-through, critical items will be missed. We cannot stress enough, the importance of walking the facility. It is impossible to see trees overhanging a fence, or a blind spot for a camera while sitting in a room somewhere else. Not all of the members need to be part of the walk-through, although it may improve the study, but the team should document the walk-through with copious digital photographs and notes to ensure that persons not present (including people reading the report later) will understand the rationale behind some of the scenarios and recommendations. All photographs and notes should be considered security-sensitive information.

Step One – Facility/Asset Characterization

Once the team has conducted all of the pre-planning and the kickoff meeting has happened, step one of the process is to

characterize the facility. Typically in Security Vulnerability Assessments, "facility characterization" means to determine all of the information about a facility that can be determined from the perspective of an adversary. Sometimes, "facility prioritization" is also included in this step, which is the process of prioritizing among multiple facilities to determine which one is most critical and vulnerable and to provide the team with an idea of which facilities need the most resources in terms of analysis and recommendations.

We recommend that the same process be used here to characterize a facility's "assets." In other words, rather than trying to analyze each one to the same level of effort, by performing a prioritization, the team can determine which assets to focus around and where to spend their effort. Note that this prioritization is not addressed by the interim final regulations or the methodology as laid out in the initial proposed regulations, so it is neither required nor prohibited. A good prioritization can save the team tens, if not hundreds, of hours which can save a company thousands of dollars. There are several different methods for prioritizing similar items, ranging from a rigorous pairwise comparison to a gut-instinct determination based on expert experience. We recommend using a semi-quantitative or at least qualitative method in order to ensure the integrity of, and ability to document, the study. In other words, if an expert tells you he or she can do it by themselves because they have tons of experience, you may be opening up your facility to liability and claims of negligence without a significant review and proof of their credentials. Even then, a more formal process is usually looked on more favorably by members of the public. The Practical Guide to Risk Management Communications lists "Use of Standards and Accepted Practices" as one of the Key Risk Issues Often of Interest to the Community.[10]

Once the team determines which assets they will focus on, it is necessary to characterize their assets. The asset characterization portion of the study includes analyzing information that describes the technical details of facility assets as required to:
- Support the analysis

---

10 Practical Guide to Risk Management Communications. p 2-9.

- Identify the potential critical assets
- Identify the hazards and consequences of concern for the facility and its surroundings and supporting infrastructure
- Identify existing layers of protection

Step	Task
Step 1: Assets Characterization	
1.1 Identify Critical Assets	Identify critical assets of the facility including people, equipment, systems, chemicals, products and information.
1.2 Identify Critical Functions	Identify the critical functions of the facility including people, equipment, systems, chemicals, products and information.
1.3 Identify Critical Infrastructure and Interdependencies	Identify the critical internal and external infrastructures and their inter-dependencies (e.g. electric power, petroleum fuels, natural gas, telecomm-unications, transportation, water, emergency services, computer systems, air handling systems, fire sys-tems, and SCADA systems) that support the critical operations of each asset.
1.4 Evaluate Existing Countermeasures	Identify what protects and supports the critical functions and assets. Identify the relevant layers of existing security systems including physical, cyber, operational administrative and business continuity planning, and the process safety systems that protect each asset.
1.5 Evaluate Impacts	Evaluate the hazards and consequences or impacts to the assets and the critical functions of the facility from the disruption, damage, or loss of each of the critical assets or functions.
1.6 Select Targets for Further Analysis	Develop a target list of critical functions and assets for further study.

Step One of the CFAT Methodology

What this means is that the team will take that technical information and try to figure out what asset the bad guys would want to attack

and what would be the consequences of them attacking it.

In a nutshell, this is the portion of the study where the company figures out which assets are: critical to their operation, could be used to impact public, or could be stolen to do harm elsewhere. These assets include: physical assets, critical personnel, information, chemicals, support processes, etc.

Asset characterization requires a macroscopic as well as a microscopic perspective of the facility or process unit being studied. It must take into consideration all aspects of the facility, from the mechanical (vessels, valves, pipes and lines) to any electronic or networked systems or controls (SCADAs, monitors, control systems, etc.) The Team must be open to all possible failure scenarios, including those thought previously untenable.

Step Two - Threat Assessment

This step involves choosing appropriate threats for the SVA based on a DHS provided Threat Assessment of the potential threats to the critical infrastructure/key resources, as well as analysis of how those threats relate to facility vulnerabilities and consequences. Note that these threats are postulated by DHS with no input from the facility itself. DHS will provide a list of Threat Scenarios based upon the type and location of the subject chemical facility. This list may vary from facility to facility. Normally during an SVA, the Threat Assessment portion of the study is where a Probability of Attack (typically called P_A) is determined. A Subject Matter Expert or team of experts uses this opportunity to develop a likelihood for each of the proposed adversaries which will be used later in calculating the risk. DHS has stated however, that "A suggested approach is to make an assumption that international terrorism is possible at every facility.[11]" What this means is that since the probability of a terrorist attack cannot be calculated, it is set to one and is therefore removed as a factor from the equation. If you choose to adopt this approach, you may need to explain to your

---

11   Chemical Facility Anti-Terrorism Standards; Proposed Rule.

management (for example) why the likelihood of attack for a single armed intruder is the same as that for a waterborne group of foreign-trained terrorists with explosives.

Since this "suggestion" from DHS is not a requirement, it does leave a facility free to develop likelihoods and we recommend a more reasonable approach which is to determine at least a "relative likelihood" for each adversary. In other words, while you might not be able to determine the real likelihood of a given adversary, you can at least rank the threats with respect to each other, and come up with a semi-quantitative way to differentiate between scenarios when developing risk later on.

There are several ways to develop this relative likelihood. Some of them are classified, some are copyrighted and others are available on the internet. The US Army uses such tools as CARVER (Criticality, Accessibility, Recognizability, Vulnerability, Effect, and Recoverability[12]) and MSHARPP (mission, symbolism, history, accessibility, recognizability, population, and proximity[13]). We have seen civilian contractors who have added additional items (called SHOCK) to the CARVER methodology to refine the results. Whatever methodology is used to develop these relative likelihoods, ensure that whomever conducts the study has the proper qualifications, uses a rigorous methodology, and follows the methodology accurately. Also, the Threat Assessment methodology needs to feed into the rest of the SVA methodology, so if the team is going to use an equation to calculate risk values, then the probabilities of attack that result need to be normalized to a value between 0 and 1 for each adversary. If the team uses a matrix to define risk values, then the team will need to use a matrix that incorporates the Probability of Attack from the Threat Assessment.

For developing a Threat Assessment, there are two kinds of information: open source, and closed source. Open source information is available to everyone via the internet, Community Right To Know, public records, etc. An excellent source of this type of information is the FBI's information sharing program:

---

12 Field Manual 34-36. Appendix D.
13   Department of Defense Dictionary of Military and Associated Terms.

Infragard. Infragard is a community of private sector individuals and companies that share information related to their sectors (Water, Chemical, Transportation, Emergency Services, etc.) They can be accessed at www.infragard.net.

Closed source information is only available to specific groups that have access to the information such as Law Enforcement, Military, etc. If you are able to access this information, please note that you will need to be careful to whom the information is disclosed. In fact, we recommend that any closed source information be kept in a separate part of the Threat Assessment.

Step Three - The Vulnerability Assessment

The actual Vulnerability Assessment portion of the study should be conducted with all of the full-time members present, and part-time members present as needed, based on their specific areas of expertise. As mentioned before, performing a Vulnerability Assessment is a structured, intensive analysis, where the Study Team examines and analyzes all aspects of a facility's assets, seeking vulnerabilities that affect the outcome of the entire study by taking into consideration possibilities not previously considered. This means that if team members are not present, there is a very good possibility that the study will be missing critical information or alternatively, that the team will have to go back and review that portion of the study for completeness and accuracy, thereby losing time and effort. For this reason, we recommend that the team be isolated from day-to-day operations (still close enough to get information if necessary) but far enough that they will not have constant interruptions.

Team Sessions

The Study Team should meet regularly (daily, if possible) until the completion of the Study. Team member attendance and

---

qualifications must be documented to ensure that it is possible to prove that the members of the team were qualified. Our team always collects a resume or biography from each team member and includes them with the rest of the documentation for the same reason. If a core team member (one of the ones legally required) cannot attend a Study Session, an alternate member must be assigned to attend. The Study Team must document their scenarios or description of impacts to assets. There should be a logical flow of ideas from beginning to end allowing anyone who reads the document – even years later – to understand what the team was discussing and how they arrived at the conclusions. Documentation can be accomplished using hand-written notes, but our teams find that it is most effective if completed through the use of a computer. To ensure that the entire team agrees upon the documentation of its discussions, we highly recommend that the session notes be entered into a computer, and the entries displayed via an overhead computer projector.

The room needs to be comfortable enough that the team can function, but should not be so comfortable that they lose focus. Refreshments/meals are done differently by different teams, but we find that foods high in sugar can produce a lethargy effect that results in loss of focus. Coffee/tea is a must. While not everyone will use them, we find that there is usually at least one member that has to have their "fix" to be able to function effectively.

It is the responsibility of the Team Leader/Facilitator to manage the schedule, and he/she should ensure that the Team is provided with periodic breaks, allowing members to refresh and re-energize themselves. While smoking is on the decline in many companies, if you have a smoker on your team, they will not be able to concentrate at all if they go too long without smoking. It is a good idea to ask at the beginning of the sessions if there are any smokers. They'll keep the team leader on track for breaks.

Members of the team may bring their own materials, but we find it helpful if each team member has their own copy of the "node documents." These are the plans, P&IDs, blueprints, etc. that the team uses to differentiate between one "node" and the next. The

Facilitator/Scribe keeps the master copy up where everyone can see them. Since the nodes are used to keep people on track, it is very useful to color them with highlighters to ensure that there is differentiation between one node and the next. If the team decides to follow this practice, then the colored drawings become a part of the permanent record of the team sessions. Other materials may include pens/pencils and paper, magnifying glasses (for hard to read documents), highlighters, binder/paper clips, removable sticky notes, etc.

Scenarios/Asset Impacts

The scenarios/asset impacts (hereafter shortened to "scenarios") need to be independent and self contained. For example, a single one should describe what happens from the adversary attack, through the results of that attack, to the risk associated with the attack, to the recommendations to prevent that attack. We recommend that all scenarios that contain references to other scenarios only refer to scenarios that have been previously discussed. In other words, if the team is discussing something that could happen in Node 5, they would not say: "We'll get to that in Node 7." They could however say: "We covered that in Node 4, so we will reference that the consequences here are the same as we already discussed." This process allows the team to ensure that they don't miss scenarios by forgetting to cover them when they get to "Node 7." One note on scenarios: if the asset based approach is used, the determination of the asset's consequences may be enough to assign a target ranking value and protect via a standard protection set for that target level. In this case, scenarios may not be developed further than the general thought that an adversary is interested in damaging or stealing an asset. Every scenario should have enough information that it can stand alone, unless it duplicates a previous scenario. Anyone who reads a scenario should have enough information from the scenario description that they will understand the

background and concerns of the team.

Causes

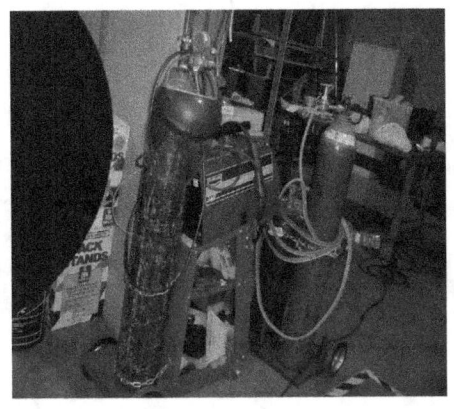

In the security world, these are the attacks carried out by the adversary. They are sometimes referred to as "initiating events." When a team performs an SVA, they list all of the relatively probable attacks that an adversary could carry out. For example, although it would be possible for an agent of an armed militia group with intentions to damage the US economy by destroying a chemical facility to carry out a graffiti attack, it is not probable. Similarly, it is unlikely that gang members would carry out an IED attack against a refinery. While DHS will be providing the threats to a chemical facility, it is unclear at this time whether those threats are just the possible adversaries or also their method of attack. If the latter is not included, then the Threat Assessment (Step 2) should be used to provide those possible attacks so that the team can proceed to list the possible consequences of each attack by a given adversary.

We recommend addressing a single adversary at a time and list all of the possible attacks, although some Facilitators will choose to address a single attack at a time and list each of the adversaries that might choose to carry out that attack. Either way is acceptable, as the most important thing when determining causes it to list all combinations of attacks that all the potential adversaries might try to carry out. Once the threats are listed, if the facility is choosing to apply a likelihood other than "1" for the Probability of Attack (P_A), then next to each cause, they can list the P_A. Table 2 is a slight modification of the table shown in the Proposed Regulations, which includes a specific adversary and the P_A for that adversary. Changes

are shown in *italics*.

Security Event Type *(Event)*	Candidate Critical Assets *(Cause)*	P_A
Ecoterrorist		
Loss of Containment, Damage, or Injury	Loss of containment of process hydrocarbons or hazardous chemicals on the plant site from intentional damage of equipment or the malicious release of process materials , which may cause multiple casualties, severe damage, and public or environmental impact. Also included is injury to personnel and the public directly or indirectly.	.5
Theft	Hydrocarbon, chemical, or information theft or misuse with the intent to cause severe harm at the facility or offsite.	.5
Contamination	Contamination or spoilage of plant products or information to cause worker or public harm on or offsite.	.5
Degradation of Assets	Degradation of assets or infrastructure or the business function or value of the facility or the entire company through destructive acts of terrorism.	.5

Table 3: Types of Security Events

Note that the P_A for the adversary is the same for every attack. While it may be possible to develop a separate P_A for each attack for each adversary, for this study we have made the assumption that the probability of the adversary attacking is a single number and that each attack is equally likely. Since the numbers are relative likelihoods rather than absolute probabilities, this assumption will still give enough gradation to be able to differentiate final risk numbers and will significantly reduce the amount of resources required to complete the Threat Assessment. Note also that for this example, we have used the probability of .5 for the adversary. This probability is not intended to indicate that in your Threat Assessment, the probability of that adversary attacking your facility is 50%. Your own probabilities will be based on factors surrounding your facility and its makeup.

Consequences

These are the results of attacks carried out by the adversary. Consequences should be detailed and should give an accurate picture of the steps that have to happen before the final consequences. As an example, rather than the scenario reading:

Cause	Consequence
Adversary destroys Tank-1 using explosives.	Potential Offsite impact resulting in over 1000 fatalities.

the scenario would read:

Cause	Consequence
Adversary destroys Tank-1 using explosives.	Processing Tower (PT-1) drains into dike through Pump (P-1). Tower overheats causing remaining gases (hydrogen, hydrogen sulfide) to catch fire and explode. Explosion releases hydrogen sulfide, hydrogen and sulfur

	dioxide to atmosphere. Potential Offsite impact resulting in over 1000 fatalities.

You can see that the second scenario gives much more detail than the first, and together with the piping and instrumentation diagrams, will give an accurate picture of the true effects of the scenario. Note that not all adversaries will have the same level of expertise and therefore should not be expected to be able to carry out the same level of consequences for a given attack however, it is common practice to take each scenario through the worst set of consequences that can result from a given event. What this means is that if this policy is followed, no safeguards are counted while developing the consequences. So the operators who will turn off the pumps, the automatic high-flow shutdowns, even the fences and cameras that will help to prevent the adversary from getting to that location are not counted to prevent the consequences from attaining their ultimate conclusions. This methodology does not mean however, that those things do not get taken into account. It simply means that they are not addressed in the consequences portion of the scenarios. They are instead addressed in the next portion of the scenario which is the "safeguards" portion.

DHS requires that the consequences of scenarios address the following items:

- Public Fatalities or Injuries
- Site Personnel Fatalities or Injuries
- Large-Scale Disruption to the National Economy, Public, or Private Operations
- Loss of Reputation or Business Viability

The Team will usually assign Severity values based upon the nature of these consequences under various Threat Scenarios (i.e.: a minor leakage of a storage vessel from a single rifle round vs. the complete rupture, evacuation and detonation of contents due to an explosive device designed specifically for that purpose.) These Severity values will be assigned based upon the Risk Matrix determined before the study began. Note that the Risk Matrix may

have a severity value for each of these categories. It is vitally important to the integrity of the study that the team not change the consequences of the scenario if they don't like the Severity value. If the team is honest with itself about the possible level of consequences, then the Severity value is based solely on those consequences – not the other way around.

Table 3 demonstrates some sample Severity values from the original proposed regulations. Note that a facility is not required by the regulations to use these severity values. When we develop a risk matrix, we always set the Severity values in decreasing order to prevent "Severity Creep." Severity Creep happens when a facility realizes that there is something more severe than their current highest Severity level, so they create a new category.

As an example, say a facility's Severity scale goes from 1-5, with 5 being their highest Severity, and a 5 represents an offsite person dying. Another regulation comes along and introduces the concept of 100 people dying offsite, so the facility creates two new Severity categories of "6," representing 10 offsite deaths, and "7," representing 100 offsite deaths. The facility goes on to do additional studies, and 5 years down the road, they have Severity categories up to "10," representing over 100,000 offsite deaths. Their risks also change with the matrix and now, a single death (which used to be the worst possible consequence) is considered an acceptable risk. We recommend that you use a Severity matrix that has a cap, but we provide this sample from the regulations for completeness.

Description	Ranking
A. Possible for any offsite fatalities from large-scale toxic or flammable release; possible for multiple onsite fatalities. B. Major environmental impact onsite and/or offsite (e.g., large-scale toxic contamination of public waterway) C. Over $X property damage D. Very long term (>X years) business interruption/expense; Large-scale disruption to the national economy, public or private operations; Loss of critical data; Loss of reputation or business viability.	S5 - Very High
A. Possible for onsite fatalities; possible offsite injuries B. Very large environmental impact onsite and/or large offsite impact C. Between $X - $Y property damage D. Long term (X months – Y years) business interruption/expense	S4 - High
A. No fatalities or injuries anticipated offsite; possible widespread onsite serious injuries B. Environmental impact onsite and/or minor impact offsite C. Between $X - $Y property damage D. Medium term (X months – Y years) business interruption/expense	S3 - Medium
A. Onsite injuries that are not widespread but only in the vicinity of the incident location; No fatalities or injuries expect offsite B. Minor environmental impacts to immediate incident site area only C. Between $X - $Y property damage D. Short term (X months – Y years) business interruption/expense	S2 - Low

Description	Ranking
A. Possible minor injury onsite; No fatalities or injuries anticipated offsite B. No environmental impacts C. Up to $X property damage D. Very short term (up to X weeks) business interruption/expense	S1 – Very Low

Table 4: Example CFAT Severity Values from the Initial Proposed Regulations

Safeguards

In the security industry, these are sometimes called "countermeasures," however the "countermeasures" that are referred to in the security industry are usually specific to security equipment that is in place to prevent theft or damage. In a safety study or an SVA, these safeguards include both things to prevent the event from taking place and things to mitigate the chain of consequences. In the example above, the fences and cameras were intended to prevent the event from ever happening, and the automatic high flow shutdown was in place to prevent the chain of events from going all the way to the final consequences. Additionally, the regulations refer to "countermeasures" as things that the team recommends to improve the facility's ability to prevent the adversary from being able to carry out an attack.

In this book, we will use the term "safeguards" for things that are in place prior to the

study to either prevent or mitigate an attack and we will use the term "recommendations" for things that the team recommends that the facility consider installing to prevent or mitigate an attack in the future. We do this for consistency's sake, (those are the terms commonly used in industry for safety studies) and to prevent confusion between the commonly used security terms, safety terms, and the current usage in the regulations.

Safeguards are the things (to include equipment, procedures, training, etc.) that prevent or mitigate events. They include the following five categories:

- Deterrence – Deterrence safeguards attempt to convince an adversary to "go somewhere else." Some argue that this just moves the risk to another location and that is all that a single facility can do. On a more macroscopic scale however, by making all of our targets harder, we will slowly make it more difficult across the board for an adversary to carry out an attack. When the cost/benefit of terrorism drops below the cost/benefit of working within the law to achieve change, we will have won. So deterrence does serve some purpose. Just remember that a sufficiently motivated adversary will never be deterred. Examples include lighting, fences, cameras, guard dogs, etc. Deterrence safeguards are required to be implemented under the DHS regulations.

- Detection – This category includes all of the methods by which a target becomes aware of an attack. The idea is to push detection out as far from the facility as possible. Our governments have several ways to detect an adversary before they even get to the facility (FBI, CIA, local law enforcement, etc.) A facility may have a neighborhood watch program with the people who live and work nearby. Cameras, when properly placed and monitored, will serve to detect an adversary. As a last resort, the employees that are at the location of the asset may detect an adversary. Detection safeguards are required to be implemented under the DHS regulations.

- Delay – Once an adversary is detected, a facility will want to delay them until the facility can respond to prevent the adversary from carrying out the attack. The rule when calculating delay time is that delay time does not begin until <u>after</u> the adversary is detected. The adversary has an unlimited amount of time in which to work until they are detected. After they are detected, then the response begins. If a facility is unable to delay the adversary until a response can be mounted, then the attack will be successful and the facility will need to mitigate the event. Some examples of delaying safeguards include: fences, K-Rail (Jersey Barriers), guard posts, checkpoints, locked doors, etc. Note that none of these items are a positive bar to entry, and many will delay an adversary only a few minutes at most. Delay safeguards are required to be implemented under the DHS regulations.

Total Time		
Working Time	Response Time	Mitigation

                            Point of   Successful

                          Detection   Attack

- Response – Response safeguards include any response that will positively stop the adversary from carrying out their attack. Note that different adversaries will be stopped by different responses. While a single unarmed guard will probably be able to stop a vandal, an armed adversary with Improvised Explosive Devices (IEDs) will need a stronger response. Examples of response safeguards include: police response, operators investigating out-of-specification parameters, private security guards checking out a sound that they heard, etc. Response safeguards are required to be implemented under the DHS regulations.
- Mitigation – Mitigation safeguards are those that help to

decrease the impact of an event if the adversary is successful in carrying out the attack. Examples include alarms (if an operator is trained and able to respond), automatic shutdowns, emergency response plans, devices that reduce the toxicity of a release such as scrubbers, devices that prevent a release from escaping (dikes, buildings, etc.), and a number of others. These recommendations are not required to be implemented under the DHS regulations however, it is prudent to take them into account for two reasons. First, the purpose of the program is to prevent the ultimate consequences of death, injury, and loss of economic capability that would come with a successful attack. If the mitigating safeguards are able to reduce the effects of the attack to negligible, then the attack is unsuccessful. Second, most recommendations tend to fall into the "delay" category, however it will be very difficult, if not impossible, to effectively delay a determined adversary. So spending most of a facility's resources on recommendations which are unlikely to be effective is lunacy.

> **Spending most of a facility's resources on recommendations which are unlikely to be effective is lunacy.**

The last thing that happens after the team lists all of the safeguards is that they determine a Likelihood for the scenario. Since the safeguards were not taken into account during the assignment of Severity, they need to be counted in this step. We typically define a Likelihood value as: "the likelihood of the stated results occurring, from the given initiating event, in spite of the listed safeguards." In other words, the Likelihood value will reflect all three elements. In an SVA methodology, our Probability of Attack (P_A) removes the probability of the initiating event from the Likelihood equation. So for this Likelihood value, we should be assuming the Probability that the given attack will be successful and result in the listed consequences in spite of the listed safeguards.

This value is called the Probability of Effectiveness (P_E.) P_E includes the adversary's capabilities and the ability of the facility to withstand an attack. It is possible to include the P_A separately from the P_E value to still have the final risk include a Probability of Attack. This inclusion can be done either through an equation or through a separate matrix from the provided Risk matrices.

Table 4 shows some sample Likelihood values based on the Initial Proposed Regulations. Again, your facility needs to use the Likelihood scale that makes sense for your situation. Note that this particular scale is similar to the provided Severity scale in that there is no "cap" on the higher end of probabilities.

Description	Probability Value[14]	Probability Value Reworded[14]	Assigned Value
Adversary is almost Certain to Succeed	0.5-1	>50/50	5
Adversary's chances of success about even	0.25-0.5	~1 in 3	4
Adversary might succeed - but less than 50/50 chance	0.125-0.25	~1 in 5	3
Adversary is probably not going to succeed	0.0625-0.125	~1 in 10	2
Extremely Unlikely	0.0312-0.0625	~1 in 20	1
Ext Impossible	<0.0312	~1 in 50	0

Table 5: Sample Likelihoods from the Initial Proposed Regulations

---

14 These descriptions are equivalent values, but different people will respond better or worse to specific wording, so both are provided.

Recommendations

Recommendations are additional safeguards that the team recommends in order to reduce the risk of an event. There are two major types of recommendations: those that reduce severity, and those that reduce likelihood. An example of a recommendation that would reduce the severity of a scenario is one that reduces the temperature and pressure of a process to reduce the effects of a release. Contrary to that example, a recommendation to add a high temperature shutdown to prevent the event from causing a failure would reduce the likelihood of the event. All recommendations can also be categorized into the 5 categories for safeguards: Deterrence, Detection, Delay, Response, and Mitigation. Remember, according to the regulations, the first four types of recommendations <u>must</u> be included in the study.

It is also possible to develop risk values for the recommendations that are associated with scenarios. The team will assign a new Severity value and Likelihood (L or P_E) value based on what would have been assigned to the scenario if the recommendation had been in place at the time of the study. This value will allow the team to see the amount of risk reduction that could be achieved by implementing a given recommendation, and management can prioritize implementation of the recommendations accordingly.

Step Four - The Risk Assessment

A risk assessment is used to determine the relative degree of risk to the facility in terms of the expected effect on each critical asset as a function of consequence and probability of occurrence. Using the assets identified during Step 1 (Asset Characterization), the scenarios are prioritized based on the Likelihood and Severity of a successful attack. The Risk of a scenario is a function of Severity and Likelihood. Once the Team has determined the values for Severity and Likelihood, the team can then determine a risk

ranking. Table 5 shows the sample risk matrix from the Initial Proposed Regulations. The values in each cell represent a degree of risk according to the scope of the study.

		Severity				
		5	4	3	2	1
Likelihood	5	High	High	High	Med	Med
	4	High	High	Med	Med	Low
	3	High	Med	Med	Low	Low
	2	Med	Med	Low	Low	Low
	1	Med	Low	Low	Low	Low

Table 6: Sample CFAT Risk Matrix from Initial Proposed Regulations

In this hypothetical risk matrix, the scope of the study may require that any event that earns a "High" ranking must be followed by a recommendation to reduce that risk ranking. Since these regulations are supposed to be risk-based, one might expect that DHS would require that the facility implement measures to reduce their risk below a certain level. What they have done instead is state that the facility must meet performance standards whether the risk is high or not. Regulatory requirements aside, the law states that the program should be risk-based so a facility needs to ensure that they follow proper risk analysis to at least prioritize their recommendations. That means that whatever matrix your facility chooses, there needs to be a level of unacceptable risk which the facility's own internal standards require that facility to mitigate to a lower risk. We also recommend against using "High", "Medium", and "Low" designations or Roman Numerals as they sort alphabetically and therefore make it more difficult to track completion of recommendations. We recommend using alphanumeric designations instead.

There is also no regulatory requirement to use a risk matrix. Although most methodologies use a matrix, the P_A, P_E, and S values can be weighted and multiplied to give a risk value. The values of each scenario can be ranked and those values can be compared to each other to determine which scenarios have the highest risk. There are two important considerations for this type of analysis. First, depending on what the S, P_A, and P_E values are, it may be difficult to set risk levels for high, medium, and low risks. The way that our team has accomplished this in the past, is by sorting all of the scenarios by risk and seeing where the natural groupings occur. There are usually between three and five major groups of scenarios and risks can be binned into those categories. The second consideration is that these values are very valuable for developing a cost-benefit analysis. Since they are actual risk values, one can mathematically use them with the cost of a given recommendation to sort recommendations based on a cost and benefit.

Countermeasures Analysis (Recommendations)

Within the DHS regulatory structure, the SVA will lead the facility directly to the production of a Site Security Plan, which must effectively address the vulnerabilities and risks identified in the Vulnerability Assessment. Accordingly, during the Vulnerability Assessment, the team must make suggested recommendations to reduce security risks. The team should develop a list of recommendations that address the security vulnerabilities that the team finds. Specifically, the team needs to make recommendations for any scenario where the risk is higher than an acceptable value (based on the facility's defined matrix.) Based on the vulnerabilities identified and the risk that the layers of security are breached, these recommendations are identified to reduce vulnerability at the facility. Some of the factors to be considered are:
- Reduced probability of successful attack (Note: this will not change the probability or risk in future updates if the DHS probability of 1 is used.)
- Degree of risk reduction resulting from each recommended

safeguard
- Reliability and maintainability of recommended safeguards
- Capabilities and effectiveness of recommended safeguards
- Costs of recommended safeguards
- Feasibility of the recommended safeguards

As mentioned before, the scenarios should be re-ranked with the recommendations to evaluate effectiveness, and prioritized to assist management in making decisions for implementing the recommended security enhancements. The recommendations should be included in a section in the Security Vulnerability Assessment report which will be used to communicate the results of the SVA to management for appropriate action.

It is the responsibility of the facility's management to receive the recommendations of the SVA team, and implement them effectively. Management must follow-up on the recommended enhancements to the security countermeasures so they are properly reviewed, tracked, and managed until they are resolved. Resolution may include adoption of the recommendations, substitution of other improvements that achieve the same level of risk abatement, or rejection. Rejection of a Vulnerability Assessment recommendation and the acceptance of the residual risk should be based on valid reasons and should be well documented.

> **COMPLETENESS CHECK: Make sure that all of the recommendations to reduce risk also meet all of the DHS performance standards.**

Interpreting the Results

Countermeasure Analysis involves determining the protective level of facility countermeasures. Countermeasures are ranked according to their ability to Deter, Detect, Delay, Respond to, or Mitigate an adversary's attempt to attack facility assets. Table 7 shows five Countermeasure Vulnerability rankings from the Initial Proposed Regulations. If these numbers are used, they must

correspond closely with the Probability of Effectiveness (P_E) values.

Vulnerability Level	Description
5 – Very High	Indicates that there are no effective protective measures currently in place to Deter, Detect, Delay, or Respond to the threat and so an adversary would easily be capable of exploiting the critical asset.
4 – High	Indicates that there are some protective measures to Deter, Detect, Delay, or Respond to the threat but not a complete or effective application of these security strategies and so it would be relatively easy for an adversary to attack the asset.
3 – Medium	Indicates that although here are some protective measures to Deter, Detect, Delay, or Respond to the threat, there is not a complete or effective application of these security strategies and so the asset or existing countermeasures could be compromised.
2 – Low	Indicates that there are effective protective measures to Deter, Detect, Delay, or Respond in place, however at least one weakness exists that an adversary would be able of exploiting with some effort to evade or defeat the countermeasure given substantial resources.
1 – Very Low	Indicates multiple layers of effective protection measures to Deter, Detect, Delay, or Respond to the threat exists, and the chances of an adversary exploiting the asset is very low.

Table 7: Sample Countermeasure Vulnerability Ranking from Initial Proposed Regulations

Documenting the Study

Documentation of the completed Vulnerability Study should include the identification of security vulnerabilities, and a set of recommendations (if necessary) to reduce risk to an acceptable level. The Vulnerability Assessment results should include a written report that documents:
- The date(s) of the study
- The study team members, their roles, expertise and experience
- A description of the scope and objectives of the study
- A description of (or reference to) the specific methodology used for the study
- The critical assets identified and the hazards and consequences associated with them
- The security vulnerabilities of the facility
- The existing countermeasures
- A set of prioritized recommendations to reduce risk

Once the report is finalized, the facility needs to implement a recommendation tracking system to ensure that the prioritized recommendations are completed in a timely manner and to document the actual resolution of each recommended action. The completed Vulnerability Assessment should contain a detailed description of the above items, properly assigned (realistic) risk rankings and recommendations to reduce those risks. The entire study should be documented in a final report form for submission to the Department of Homeland Security, and to facility management for recommendation implementation.

Security Sensitive Information

The information that is developed as a part of the SVA is security-sensitive information. In fact, it is so sensitive, that DHS has created a new classification of information: Chemical Terrorism Vulnerability Information (CVI). This new classification is similar

to SECRET, NOFORN, CLASSIFIED, etc. Most of the regulations apply to government employees who need to have access to the information, but some of the concerns apply to state and local officials who also need to have access to the information, and the facility will have certain responsibilities to keep this information safe as well.

Facilities are responsible for determining which information falls under the category of CVI and for marking their CVI so that it is not accidentally disclosed. The hardest part for facilities will be in determining which of their information actually falls under this regulation and which does not. For example, much Risk Management Plan information is accessible to the public under the Freedom of Information Act, (FOIA) but if that information is also used to help develop an SVA, does it then become CVI and therefore exempt from disclosure? DHS has not clarified these conundrums yet, so it will behoove a company to pay very close attention to what they declare as CVI. Note too, that while CVI will not be released as public information, the company will assume the responsibility of ensuring that the information is kept safe. We recommend having the company's lawyers take a look at the information before classifying it either way and work together with the team leader to determine what will be considered CVI and what will not. The following information is considered CVI:

- Security Vulnerability Assessments
- Site Security Plans
- Documents relating to the Department's review and approval of Security Vulnerability Assessments and Site Security Plans, including Letters of Authorization, Letters of Approval and responses thereto; written notices; and other documents developed for these items
- Alternate Security Programs
- Documents relating to SVA inspection or audits
- Any records required to be created or retained under the regulations
- Sensitive portions of orders, notices or letters from DHS issued under the regulations

- Information developed about a facility's level of risk
- Other information developed for chemical facility security purposes that the Secretary, in his discretion, determines is similar to the other information protected in the regulations and which thus warrants protection as CVI.

The following marking has to be put on the top of the cover (front and back), the title page and each page:

CHEMICAL TERRORISM VULNERABILITY INFORMATION

The following distribution limitation statement has to be put on the bottom of the cover (front and back), the title page and each page:

> **WARNING: This record contains Chemical-terrorism Vulnerability Information controlled by 6 CFR 27.400. Do not disclose to persons without a "need to know" in accordance with 6 CFR 27.400(e). Unauthorized release may result in civil penalties or other action. In any administrative or judicial proceeding, this information shall be treated as classified information in accordance with 6 CFR 27.400(h) and (i).**

For non-paper documents, the regulations state:

> In the case of non-paper records that contain CVI, including motion picture films, videotape recordings, audio recording, and electronic and magnetic records, a covered person must clearly and conspicuously mark the records with the protective marking and the distribution limitation statement such that the viewer or listener is reasonably likely to see or hear them when obtaining access to the contents of the record.

The regulations require the following people to protect CVI:[15],[16],[17],[18]

- Each person who has a need to know CVI. These people:
  - Require access to specific CVI to carry out chemical facility security activities approved, accepted, funded, recommended, or directed by DHS.
  - Need the information to receive training to carry out chemical facility security activities approved, accepted, funded, recommended, or directed by DHS.
  - Need the information to supervise or otherwise manage individuals carrying out chemical facility security activities approved, accepted, funded, recommended, or directed by DHS.
  - Need the information to provide technical or legal advice to a covered person, who has a need to know the information, regarding chemical facility security requirements of Federal law.
  - Are determined by DHS that access is required under the regulations in the course of a judicial or administrative proceeding.
  - Are Federal employee who need access to the information for performance of the employee's official duties.
  - Acting in the performance of a contract with or grant from DHS, if access to the information is necessary to

15   Need to know may be further limited by DHS. For some specific CVI, DHS may make a finding that only specific persons or classes of persons have a need to know.

16   Nothing in Sec. 27.400(e) shall prevent DHS from determining, in its discretion, that a person not otherwise listed in Sec. 27.400(e) has a need to know CVI in a particular circumstance.

17   DHS may require that non-Federal persons seeking access to CVI complete a non-disclosure agreement before such access is granted.

18   DHS may make an individual's access to the CVI contingent upon satisfactory completion of a security background check or other procedures and requirements for safeguarding CVI that are satisfactory to the Department.

performance of the contract or grant. Contractors or grantees may not further disclose CVI without the consent of the Assistant Secretary.

- Each person who otherwise receives or gains access to what they know or should reasonably know constitutes CVI.

People who are required to protect the information have to

- Take reasonable steps to safeguard CVI in that person's possession or control, including electronic data, from unauthorized disclosure. When a person is not in physical possession of CVI, the person must store it in a secure container, such as a safe, that limits access only to covered persons with a need to know.
- Disclose, or otherwise provide access to, CVI only to persons who have a need to know.
- Refer requests for CVI by persons without a need to know to the Assistant Secretary.
- Mark CVI as specified in the regulations.
- Dispose of CVI as specified in the regulations.
- If a covered person receives a record or verbal transmission containing CVI that is not marked as specified in the regulations, they must:
  - Mark the record as specified in the regulations.
  - Inform the sender of the record that the record must be marked as specified in the regulations.
  - Or, if received

Chemical Facility
XXX

Security Vulnerability Assessment

CHEMICAL TERRORISM VULNERABILITY INFORMATION

WARNING: This record contains Chemical-terrorism Vulnerability Information controlled by 6 CFR 27.400. Do not disclose to persons without a "need to know" in accordance with 6 CFR 27.400(e). Unauthorized release may result in civil penalties or other action. In any administrative or judicial proceeding, this information shall be treated as classified information in accordance with 6 CFR 27.400(h) and (i).

verbally, make reasonable efforts to memorialize such information and mark the memorialized record as specified in the regulations, and then inform the speaker of any determination that such information warrants CVI protection.

- If someone required to protect the information becomes aware that CVI has been released to someone that shouldn't have access, they have to promptly inform the Assistant Secretary.

DHS has developed online training for authorized users. The Chemical-Terrorism Vulnerability Information (CVI) Authorized User Training can be found at: http://www.dhs.gov/xlibrary/assets/training/cvi/_frameset.htm.

Chapter

4

The Site Security Plan (SSP)
Developing The SSP

Step Five – Risk Reduction

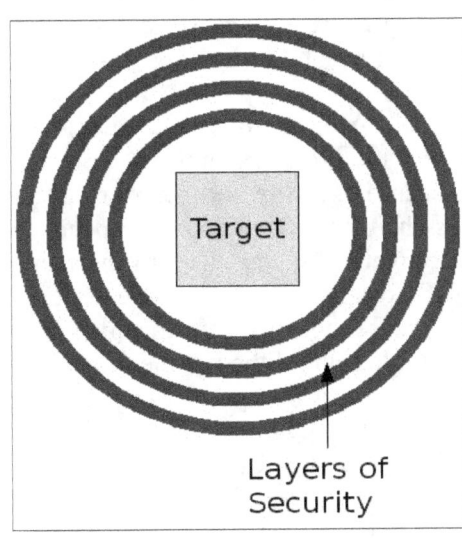

Once facility management has a comprehensive under-standing of the facility's vulnerabilities, it can then proceed to the next step of the process, which is to develop an effective Site Security Plan (SSP) which is one of the key measures in a facility's defense against an attack. This plan highlights the measures a facility has imple mented to reduce the chance of a successful terrorist strike.

According to the regulations, DHS will provide site assistance visits to facilities who appear to be at a higher risk of

terrorist attack (most likely Tiers 1 and 2). DHS will also conduct these visits upon the request of the owner. These visits are conducted by DHS protective security professionals and/or subject matter experts, as well as by local law enforcement, with the goal of identifying vulnerabilities and discussing options for mitigation. The goal of these visits is to produce information aimed at bolstering the facility's defenses against terrorist attack. There is no deadline in the regulations for when DHS will conduct these visits, nor is there any protocol listed for how to make the request, when the information will be provided back etc. We believe that the facility is probably on its own for a while.

The Site Security Plan should create a layered defensive perimeter for the facility. It must address the SVA findings, as well as applicable "risk-based performance standards" from DHS. In the case of Vulnerability Assessment findings, the SSP addresses the ways in which the facility corrects its identified vulnerabilities. "Risk-based performance standards" are generated by DHS, and can vary from facility to facility. Typically, however, these standards will require a facility's Site Security Plans to develop and explain security measures to:

- **Secure and monitor the perimeter of the facility** – it is unclear whether this means that (for example) a farm using ammonia will need to secure its entire perimeter or only the part with the hazardous chemical. DHS does not specify the extent of the facility perimeter, leaving it up to the facility themselves. While DHS does not specify the threats against which the facility must secure the perimeter, they do specify that the facility must be able to hold the perimeter against a threat until a response can be put into place. This is one of the more difficult aspects of the regulation as most facilities want to comply with the standards, but securing the perimeter against an armed group of religious terrorists with paramilitary training will require a more robust defense than securing the perimeter against a single adversary with no training who has a gripe against management. Unless DHS specifies in its guidance document what level of protection

is required, your company will have to set up its own internal standards that it will have to meet for this item and the rest.

- **Secure and monitor restricted areas or potentially critical targets within the facility** – this standard has a similar failing to the previous bullet: it is difficult to tell what a facility has to do to meet this standard. What the regulations mean by "monitor" is unclear as well. There has, to date, been no guidance on how often these areas

need to be visited or viewed in order to "monitor" them.

- **Control access to the facility and to restricted areas within the facility by screening and/or inspecting individuals, deliveries, and vehicles as they enter; including:**
    - **Measures to deter the unauthorized introduction of dangerous substances and devices that may facilitate an attack or actions having serious negative consequences for the population**

surrounding the facility – These measures could include inspections of vehicle under carriages, trunks, gloveboxes, etc. We recommend using a standard protocol for inspecting every vehicle. The level of inspection should vary depending on the threat level.

- **Measures implementing a regularly updated identification system that checks the identification of facility personnel and other persons seeking access to the facility and that discourages abuse through established disciplinary measures** – We recommend one of the standard badging systems that has a recognizable photo of the employee and is required to be visible while the employee is on the facility premises. Employees should also be instructed to remove the badge when not on the premises to prevent potential adversaries from learning what the badges look like and duplicating them.

- **Deter vehicles from penetrating the facility perimeter, gaining unauthorized access to restricted areas or otherwise presenting a hazard to potentially critical targets** – Typically, implementation of this measure involves the use of fences, walls, K-Rail (Jersey Barriers) and guards. An onsite driving policy also helps to keep vehicles below speed limits and away from critical areas.

- **Secure and monitor the shipping and receipt of hazardous materials from the facility** – The US Department of Transportation (DOT) already has regulations detailing the responsibilities of Hazardous Materials shippers with regard to protecting them from terrorists (HM-222). In the absence of clarifying guidance on this topic from DHS, if a facility complies with the requirements of the HM-222 regulations, and incorporates them into their SSP, they should meet the requirements of this section.

- **Deter theft or diversion of potentially dangerous chemicals** – While most facilities currently have loss prevention programs in place, we recommend enhancing the loss prevention program to specifically call out these chemicals and take extra steps to ensure that they are not stolen and used against other targets.
- **Deter insider sabotage** – The most common forms of implementing this measure are background checks and prevention of workplace violence programs. While these programs do not directly prevent sabotage, the first will both help to identify some possible threats and let employees know that the company is taking steps to prevent hiring employees that might be a threat. The second lets employees know that the facility is watching for signs of suspicious behavior. The major flaw in these programs is that "moles," or people who pretend to be employees in order to sabotage a plant are instructed and trained to blend in with the other employees and so neither a background check or a workplace violence program is likely to catch those threats. The facility will need to develop separate measures to prevent opportunities for sabotage as much as prevent saboteurs from entering the facility.
- **Deter cyber-sabotage, including by preventing unauthorized on site or remote access to critical process controls, Supervisory Control And Data Acquisition (SCADA) systems, and other sensitive computerized systems** – The first thing that a facility needs to do to to protect its cyber-assets is to physically secure the equipment. The second thing is to institute good cyber-security systems such as firewalls, procedures, administrators who know how to recognize intrusions, etc.
- **Develop and exercise an emergency plan to respond to security incidents internally and with assistance of local law enforcement and first responders** – Every facility should have an emergency response plan (ERP), a business continuity plan (BCP) or Continuity of Operations Plan

(COOP), and a plan for interfacing with their local jurisdiction. Having said that, most facilities do not have these plans. And the emergency plans that most facilities do have are not complete enough to actually list the steps that the facility must complete when an emergency does happen. Many times, ERPs are something that a facility develops and then puts on a shelf. To be fair, most companies have no experience developing ERPs, and they have other priorities. (e.g. making chemicals or other products) Once an emergency does occur however, they are at the mercy of the event. The ERPs required under the SVA regulations are different than the ERPs that a facility is used to developing. They require interfacing with local law enforcement and emergency responders, which may be difficult to do. DHS has not provided guidance on what a facility is to do if local law enforcement or emergency response personnel are unable or unwilling to participate in developing and exercising the plans. We recommend that if the facility cannot secure the assistance of law enforcement or emergency preparedness personnel in developing their ERP, that the facility provide a copy of their ERP to both departments when completed.

- **Maintain effective monitoring, communications and warning systems, including:**
    - **Measures designed to ensure that security systems and equipment are in good working order and inspected, tested, calibrated, and otherwise maintained**
    - **Measures designed to regularly test security systems, note deficiencies, correct for detected deficiencies, and record results so that they are available for inspection by DHS**
    - **Measures to allow the facility to promptly identify and respond to security system and equipment failures or malfunctions**
  – These are no different than the maintenance programs that

most facilities have in place for maintaining their operational equipment. The same type of programs need to be in place for security equipment to ensure that it stays functional and will actually work to prevent or mitigate an attack.

- **Ensure proper security training, exercises, and drills of facility personnel** – DHS has not specified in the regulations what "proper" means in this bullet. However, just as employees need to be trained and practice to ensure that they know how to operate their equipment properly, they also need to be trained to respond properly in an emergency. Upon hiring, every employee should at least get a basic awareness of their function if an emergency happens, and how the overall organization intends to respond. Annual refresher training should also be held, along with exercises to test whether the plan works and employees both know their functions and can carry it out. DHS does not specify how often these exercises must be held to comply with the regulations; most agencies conduct exercises between quarterly and annually.

- **Perform appropriate background checks on and ensure appropriate credentials for facility personnel, and as appropriate, for unescorted visitors with access to restricted areas or potentially critical targets** – DHS specifically calls out background checks in the regulations and states that proper background checks need to include measures that verify and validate identity, check criminal history, and verify/validate an employee's legal authorization to work. There is no guidance from DHS on specific services to use for background checks or other measures.

- **Escalate the level of protective measures for periods of elevated threat** – The facility will need to develop their SSP to include measures of protection that increase with the threat level. What this means is that the facility cannot simply set their measures of protection and let them sit.

They will need to develop separate sets of measures for each level. For example, at the yellow threat level, the facility may require all guests to be escorted by the person they are visiting, at the orange level, guests may be restricted in the areas that they can visit even with an escort, and at red, the facility may deny visits to all guests.

- **Address specific threats, vulnerabilities, or risks identified by the Assistant Secretary for the particular facility at issue** – The Assistant Secretary may provide a list of specific threats to the facility and the facility will need to address those specific threats.

- **Report significant security incidents to the Department** – DHS has not provided any guidance on what constitutes a "significant" security incident. We recommend having all employees view the video "The Seven Signs of Terrorism", created by Michigan's State Police to help them decide what is a "significant" event. The video is available for download from our website: http://www.oursafetowns.com/resources.htm, and explains many ways that people can recognize an adversary doing their research in preparation for an attack. Additionally, there are a number of other materials available (both free and for sale) to help a facility train their employees how to recognize a potential threat. Once the facility determines what needs to be reported to DHS however, there is still the need to actually report it. DHS has not set up a method by which the facility can report incidents to DHS yet, so hopefully, that information will be forthcoming.

- **Identify, investigate, report, and maintain records of significant security incidents and suspicious activities in or near the site** – As mentioned before, DHS has not stipulated what "significant" incidents are. Once the facility determines what to define as a "significant" security incident, the facility will need to ensure that they document these incidents and investigate them. DHS has also not specified how long the facility will need to maintain these

records. Note however, that records of security incidents will need to be marked and treated as CVI.

- **Establish official(s) and an organization responsible for security and for compliance with these standards** – Similar to safety regulations, the company must designate someone within the organization to be responsible for ensuring that the regulations are carried out and that the program is being properly implemented. This is the person who is responsible for the entire program and certifies that it is sufficient and complete to DHS. We sometimes refer to this person as "the one who goes to jail if they're lying." The responsibility is significant and should not be delegated below the level of corporate director. Typically, security organizations recommend that the person responsible for security have a direct line to the CEO or president. In practice, this responsibility is sometimes delegated to a lower level, but that level should still be able to obligate corporate resources for carrying out the recommendations of the SVA team. In addition to the individual responsible for the program, if the company designates additional personnel to be responsible for portions of the program, then those personnel should be organized into either functional or geographic responsibilities, and assigned both responsibility for, and authority to, carry out assigned functions.

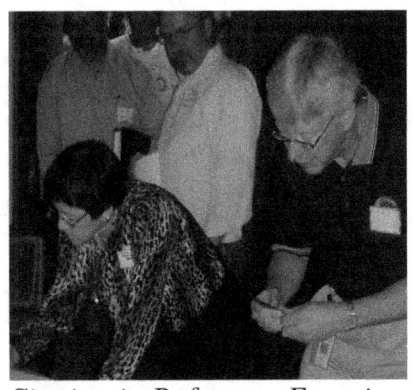

Signing in Before an Exercise

- **Maintain appropriate records** – In Section 27.255 of the regulations, DHS states that a facility needs to maintain the following records for 3 years and make them available to DHS on request:

- Training –
  - Date of each session
  - Location of each session
  - Time of day
  - Duration of session
  - Description of the training
  - Name and qualifications of the instructor
  - Clear, legible list of attendees to include the attendee signature
  - At least one other unique identifier of each attendee receiving the training
  - The results of any evaluation or testing.
- Drills and exercises
  - Date held
  - Description of the drill or exercise
  - List of participants
  - List of equipment (other than personal equipment) tested or employed in the exercise
  - Name(s) and qualifications of the exercise director
  - Any best practices or lessons learned which may improve the Site Security Plan
- Incidents and breaches of security
  - Date of occurrence
  - Time of occurrence
  - Location within the facility
  - Description of the incident or breach
  - Identity of the individual to whom it was reported
  - Description of the response
- Maintenance, calibration and testing of security equipment, for each occurrence:
  - Date
  - Time
  - Name/Qualifications of the technician(s) doing the work
  - Specific security equipment involved
- Security Threats (bomb, chemical, or biological threats,

facility surveillance, etc.)
- Date of occurrence
- Time of occurrence
- How the threat was communicated
- Who received or identified the threat
- Description of the threat
- To whom the threat was reported
- Description of the response
- Audit Records
  - Date of the audit
  - Results of the audit
  - Name(s) of the person(s) who conducted the audit
  - Letter certified by the covered facility stating the date the audit was conducted
- Letters of Authorization and Approval
  - Documentation identifying the results of audits and inspections conducted

DHS also states that a facility needs to maintain the following records for 6 years and make them available to DHS on request:
- Top-Screen information
- SVA
- SSP

While DHS states that these records can be kept in electronic format, electronic records must be protected against unauthorized access, deletion, destruction, amendment, and disclosure.

- **Address any additional performance standards the Assistant Secretary may specify** – DHS may choose to create additional performance standards nation-wide based on additional threat information, or may specify standards for individual facilities above and beyond those designated for other facilities. The facility will need to treat these specific requirements with the same level of vigor as the generic requirements that they are currently required to implement as DHS is expected to inspect/audit them at least

as stringently as any others.

Countermeasure Consideration: Cost Vs. Benefit

Once vulnerabilities have been identified, and recommendations have been made, the facility management must determine the most cost-effective means to implement countermeasures. In this section, a number of determining factors are discussed regarding possible solutions to this dilemma. Safeguards usually fall into the same categories as in the safety field: Personal Protective Equipment (PPE), Engineering Controls and Personnel Controls. Note that the sections below only describe a couple of the more common recommendations. One of the members of your team should be a trained security professional who has proper knowledge of security design and operation in order to determine the right recommendations for a given facility. They should work closely with your management, operations, and safety personnel to ensure that the right combination of safeguards is developed to provide the best security, safety and operational posture for the facility. Any recommendations developed in a vacuum, that is, without the input from all of these parties, may conflict with other goals that the company wants to achieve. As an example, many fire departments require panic hardware and/or access controls that present opportunities for adversaries to access the facility. While a security expert will want to do away with that equipment, they legally cannot do so, and if the company's overall goal in these programs is to preserve life, they should not do so. Be especially careful to ensure that these issues are resolved if your company retains outside expertise for these recommendations. Otherwise, your expert may already be gone when you find out that none of their recommendations can be implemented.

Personal Protective Equipment

Personal Protective Equipment is often used in the safety field to protect body parts against flying debris or chemicals. Examples include protective eyewear, latex gloves, rubber aprons, and steel toed boots. In the security field, PPE includes shooting glasses and gloves, bomb suits, armored vests, vehicle armor, etc. Very few, if any, recommendations from your SVA on a chemical facility will be PPE recommendations.

Engineering Controls

Engineering controls are so called because they "engineer" the problem out of the system, not because they require engineering design or are designed by engineers. Examples from the safety field include guards on cutting machinery or dykes to reduce the surface area of a release. Engineering controls in the security field will include cameras, locks, doors, barriers, etc. When developing recommendations to minimize the risk to a facility, a combination of security and safety recommendations should be considered. For example, a defense-in-depth plan for preventing an adversary from carrying out an attack to cause a tank explosion is a good safeguard, but you may also include recommendations to reduce the pressure in the tank, reinforce the tank, provide more relief capacity and more. This combination of recommendations – a whole system view – will provide the most complete and cost-effective solution to the gaps in your current security strategy.

Engineering Controls: High Tech = High Cost

While this subtitle is not always true, as a general rule, technology increases the cost to a facility rather than decreases the cost. Many people think that they can leverage technology to reduce

their security costs. This concept is true – up to a point. When discussing introducing <u>new</u> security capabilities however, the technological solution is probably one of the more expensive solutions. While high-tech solutions can be used as a force multiplier, (e.g. cameras to reduce the number of guards required to patrol an area) it will not eliminate the cost of someone to monitor those cameras. And cameras have to be monitored effectively in order to detect an adversary which means that a human needs to be viewing them on a regular schedule.

Some examples of high-tech recommendations include:

Cameras

Cameras can be an effective method for a relatively small number of security persons to maintain surveillance on a large area. A well planned camera system may allow unauthorized act-ivity/intruders to be detected quickly. Such a system can pinpoint the loc-ation of threats,

Typical Security Cameras

allowing a security force to effectively maneuver in response to the threat. Even the implication that an area is under camera surveillance can contribute to increased security (e.g. dummy cameras,) but be aware that dummy cameras may actually increase a company's liability if employees and/or the public have an expectation that they are being monitored. In the past, persons who have been attacked while "under observation" from a dummy camera, have sued companies stating that they believed that they would be safe in that area since they had an expectation that someone would see them in the camera and would respond.

Major weaknesses of camera systems include the power source and data recording systems. Cameras can be blocked, disabled, or spoofed. (e.g. an intruder transmits what appears to be an unaffected space to the control center, while there is illicit activity taking place.) In addition, the effectiveness of a camera system relies on the personnel monitoring the system.

A human monitored control room.

Another concern for camera effectiveness is the lighting level required by the specific camera type and model. While night-vision and infrared cameras are available, they cost much more than comparable regular light cameras – for regular cameras, you will need to take into account the power requirements for lighting when calculating the costs of implementation. Even when you have taken all of the lighting, placement, and field of view, etc. requirements into account, camera resolution will be a concern. If the resolution is not fine enough, then you will be unable to see enough detail to distinguish friends and foes, and you will not be able to identify an adversary for identification later.

Alarm Systems

Monitored alarm systems can also be an effective method of detection. The simplest monitoring systems feed a signal from the alarm being monitored to a central monitoring station, where humans interpret the signal and interpret the condition of the monitored unit.

As alarm systems increase in sophistication, the incoming data signals are more and more often routed through a computerized control system. This system may expand to include automatic control logic that activates safety interlocks and optimally, performs safe shutdown procedures. The system may also activate warning messages that are sent to the appropriate responders assigned to protect the facility.

Electronic Access Systems

Both key card and proximity card access systems provide a sophisticated (but passive) intruder deterrence and denial system. The most basic system reads data from a card carried by an authorized employee and opens the lock to allow access. One advantage of this type of system is that every time a lock is opened, the system can log it and so provide security with a trail of where the employee's card has been used. A second advantage is that every card can be separately programmed to allow personnel to open specific locks while preventing

Key Card System

78

them from opening others. This system allows a facility to provide layered protection around critical assets. A third advantage is that the employee's card can (in very high-end systems) be tailored to include the use of a biometric identification system to confirm that the key card is being used by an authorized person.

One weakness of this system is that it requires the employee to protect his/her issued card from unauthorized use. Another is that the system requires electrical power to operate correctly. When designing a security system of this type, a significant level of effort is required to ensure that the right level of access is provided for each employee.

Information Technology

Attacks from hackers and cyber-criminals can be minimized through the use of firewalls and data access controls. An effective and trained IT Department, combined with effective IT policies and equipment can reduce the likelihood that a facility will suffer loss from a cyber attack. While the proper training and equipment will be dependent on the threat at any given time, proper policies and procedures will include password protection along with requirements on password length, special characters, frequency of changes, number of times a new password is required before one can be repeated, etc. Good policies will also include the frequency of virus scanning, how often the virus scanning software is updated, and what personal software that employees can install on their own computers. IT policies should also take into account the new software that people need to install to get their jobs done (in a high-tech world, the right tool may mean the difference between success and failure) and balance that need with the requirement to

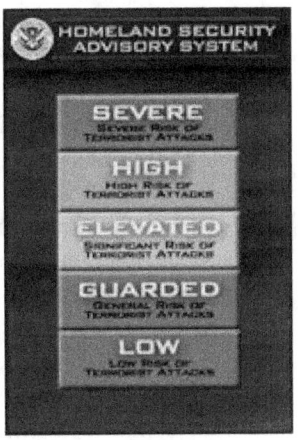

prevent Trojan horses from being installed on the network.

Wikipedia[19] has the following to say about computer viruses:

> A computer virus is a computer program that can copy itself and infect a computer without permission or knowledge of the user. The original may modify the copies or the copies may modify themselves, as occurs in a metamorphic virus. A virus can only spread from one computer to another when its host is taken to the uninfected computer, for instance by a user sending it over a network or carrying it on a removable medium such as a floppy disk, CD, USB drive or by the Internet. Additionally, viruses can spread to other computers by infecting files on a network file system or a file system that is accessed by another computer. Viruses are sometimes confused with computer worms and Trojan horses. A worm, however, can spread itself to other computers without needing to be transferred as part of a host. A Trojan horse is a file that appears harmless until executed. In contrast to viruses, Trojan horses do not insert their code into other computer files.
>
> Many personal computers are now connected to the Internet and to local area networks, facilitating the spread of malicious code. Today's viruses may also take advantage of network services such as the World Wide Web, e-mail, and file sharing systems to spread, blurring the line between viruses and worms. Furthermore, some sources use an alternative terminology in which a virus is any form of self-replicating malware.

---

19 Wikipedia: Computer virus

The term comes from the term virus in biology. A computer virus reproduces by making (possibly modified) copies of itself in the computer's memory, storage, or over a network. This is similar to the way a biological virus works.

Some viruses are programmed to damage the computer by damaging programs, deleting files, or reformatting the hard disk. Others are not designed to do any damage, but simply replicate themselves and perhaps make their presence known by presenting text, video, or audio messages. Even these benign viruses can create problems for the computer user. They typically take up computer memory used by legitimate programs. As a result, they often cause erratic behavior and can result in system crashes. In addition, many viruses are bug-ridden, and these bugs may lead to system crashes and data loss.

There are many viruses operating in the general Internet today, and new ones are created and discovered every day.

Engineering Controls: Low Tech = Low Cost

Again, low tech is not always equal to low cost, but in general, if properly implemented, solutions that require low technology also require less capital. These solutions range from barriers, to locks and doors, to lighting, to proper layout of the space to be defended.

Barriers

Barriers are the least expensive method of deterrent and denial with some measure of effectiveness. Note that no barrier can be considered a positive bar to entry (e.g. A fence is not expected to last more than a few seconds against all but the most inept of adversaries. A

Chain Link Fencing Topped With Barbed Wire

simple chain link fence around a facility serves to keep out the curious and low-threat intruders, such as vandals and persons seeking secluded locations for illicit purposes. The simple presence of a fence implies a certain authority over an area, a subtle warning for the general public to keep out. When located inside a facility, it provides an obvious indication that only authorized persons are allowed inside the fence (for example, an area with high voltage equipment that should only be accessed by electricians). A chain link fence topped with barbed or razor wire increases the warning, and may be effective in deterring less determined intruders.

In addition to chain link fencing, there are many other types

Jersey Barriers (K-Rail)

of fencing that are appropriate for use in an industrial facility. Close mesh fencing is more difficult to climb than chain link, and chain link with a finer mesh wire (chicken wire) attached to the outside may also deter climbers. In areas where fencing is considered unsightly, the facility may choose to use wrought iron fencing, but be advised that the cost will go up significantly.

Double fence lines present a more forceful message but may attract more attention from the curious. A properly designed double fence provides a number of advantages, such as a buffer zone between fences, increasing the likelihood that an intruder's presence will be detected while he or she attempts to negotiate the inner fence line. This space also lends itself to various detection systems, providing a zone where only authorized persons are found, and whose movements are coordinated with a central security authority. For specific design and installation standards for fences, consult the <u>Protection Of Assets Manual</u>, published by the American Society for Industrial Security (the same professional organization that certifies protection professionals.)

Barriers may also deter larger threats, such as vehicles, watercraft, and aircraft. Normally used for highway lane restrictions, concrete Jersey barriers (K-Rail) can be used to prevent straight-line vehicle access to a facility. This technique of placing Jersey barriers in alternating locations along a road prevents a vehicle from accelerating, deny it the opportunity to gain velocity and momentum to penetrate through a gate or access way.

Other barrier systems include concrete planters, used to deny access to areas of concern to both vehicles and crowds, while simultaneously making the appearance of the perimeter of the area seem less sterile by beautifying the protective measures. Aerial barriers, such as helicopter denial  *Concrete Planters*

wires (high-tensile wires strung from poles above a protected area which are designed to interfere with a helicopter's rotor blades) may deter an assault from helicopter borne assailants.

Barriers may also be used to help protect structures from various weapons systems. Cladding a storage vessel in simple chain link fencing has been used successfully to detonate an armor piercing rocket before it actually strikes its target. In its dealings with the Irish Republican Army (IRA) terrorists, the British Army Engineers used this method to protect important buildings. A variation of this defense is used for U.S. Army Stryker[20] vehicles today.

Illustration 1: A U.S. Army Stryker vehicle with rocket denial armor

Locks

One of the oldest security systems still in use today is the lock. Locks deny easy access to spaces. Although individual locks

---

20 US Army Fact File: Stryker.

are not considered to be a positive bar to entry, when combined with an active security program and key control system, the use of locks can be an effective passive denial system. Employing an effective key control system allows a facility to maintain a continuous security posture for low cost. The primary drawback to a lock-dependent system is a requirement for strict key accountability; should a key to a security area come up missing, the cost to replace all of the affected locks can build quickly.

There are several different types of locks and a good locksmith can recommend the right kind for your facility. They may even recommend a Master Key System for opening multiple locks with a single key. Similar to a key card system, a Master Key System will allow multiple tiers of management to open progressively more sensitive areas. While a key card system is much more configurable (each key can be separately programmed) and the loss of a key may mean the compromise of the entire system, these Master Key Systems can be an effective way to develop layers of security around sensitive areas.

Personnel Controls – No Tech

There are several measures that can be implemented by a company that will improve security and safety but which require little or no hardware. This section will describe a few of them as examples, but cannot possibly serve as a comprehensive reference of all the possible solutions that can be implemented at a given facility. These solutions should be used in conjunction with engineering controls. Note that personnel controls alone are never considered to be sufficient – some engineering controls will be necessary to protect your facility.

Policies and Procedures

Policies and procedures are the bane of any recommendation plan. They can be cumbersome, require changes to perfectly good

operations, and can be difficult to implement. Employees must be trained in the procedures, and the company will need to periodically follow up to ensure that the employees are actually following the policies and procedures. Having said that, they can be the most cost effective way to implement portions of your security program, they can save lives on the safety side, and if properly designed, can even improve a facility's processes.

An example of using policies and procedures to enhance a company's security preparedness is a facility's hiring practices. Employee hiring processes may provide a deterrent to intruders and attackers by incorporating background checks and employee screening. Another is a company's disciplinary processes. Policies/ procedures outlining proper employee conduct will do a great deal towards reducing a facility's vulnerability to hostile activities. Good policies and procedures have the following characteristics:

- They are understandable (and understood) by the workforce.
- They are enforceable (and enforced) by management.
- No one is exempt (even the CEO gets his bags screened).
- They are not easily circumvented.
- There are no conflicting rules (e.g. safety versus security rules.)
- They do not cause a significant impact on work (e.g. If a person has to go through 16 doors to get back into the building after a smoke break, they are more likely to prop open the emergency exit.)

While good policies and procedures may be difficult to create and implement, the rewards in the long run are significant. They can reduce equipment costs, preserve life and equipment, and reduce liability. At a minimum, a facility's policies should include:

- Authorities for the Policies
- Purpose in implementing the Policies
- The company's position on deviations from a policy (penalties for deviation without authorization)
- Who is authorized to implement a deviation from a policy

- Who has authority in an emergency (corporate or government)
- Anything that the facility needs to set to paper to ensure that employees understand what management's position is on a particular topic.

Similar to policies, a company will need procedures to implement those policies. These procedures will include human resources procedures, information technology procedures, operating procedures, maintenance procedures, safety procedures, security procedures, and emergency response procedures. While procedures do not always need to be in writing, the DHS regulations require written procedures, and implementation of an unwritten procedure is incredibly difficult to document. At a minimum, the list of a facility's procedures should include the following:

- Human Resources Procedures:
  - Hiring
  - Firing, Layoffs, Resignations
  - Workplace Violence
  - Background Checks
  - Lifestyle Changes (for critical employees)
  - Cash/Payroll
- Information Technology Procedures:
  - Responsible Use of Company Assets (computers, internet, email, etc.)
  - Password Procedures
  - Physical Security of Servers
  - Backups
- Operating Procedures:
  - Operations Personnel Qualifications
  - Startup
  - Shutdown
  - Emergency Shutdown
  - Deviation from Normal Conditions
- Maintenance Procedures (including Security Equipment):
  - Maintenance Personnel Qualifications
  - Frequency of Inspection, Calibration and Maintenance

- • Allowable Substitutions for Replacement-In-Kind
  - • Management of Change and Pre-Startup Safety Reviews (If the facility falls under the PSM, RMP or similar State Regulations)
- • Safety Procedures:
  - • OSHA requirements
  - • Ergonomics
  - • Fire Prevention/Protection
- • Security Procedures (note that the regulations require security procedures to change with an increase in the Terrorist Threat):
  - • Badging
  - • Entry to/Exit from the Facility
  - • Visitors (escorts, etc.)
  - • Use of Cameras
  - • Guards (rounds, frequency, posts, post orders, checkpoints, etc.)
- • Emergency Response Procedures
  - • Egress
  - • Accountability
  - • Business Continuity

Buffer Zone Protection Program (BZPP)

In 2005, the Department of Homeland Security announced $91.3 million in grant funding to protect and secure areas

surrounding critical infrastructure and key resource sites such as chemical facilities, dams, and nuclear plants across the country. The Buffer Zone Protection Program (BZPP) provides targeted funding through states to local jurisdictions to purchase equipment that will extend the zone of protection beyond the gates of these critical facilities. This program is designed for the facility to work with its neighbors to deter and detect threats before they ever get to the

facility. As an example, if the facility next door has a security guard and your facility has a security guard who each make periodic rounds but need to have someone at their post while making rounds, then the two companies might be able to arrange to have the guards cover each other's posts while the other one makes the rounds of his facility, thereby saving each company the cost of another guard.

Architecture

Architectural techniques can be used that incorporate both physical and psychological intruder deterrents; a building that looks impregnable is less likely to be considered a target for intruders. Designing a layered passive defense design that channels foot traffic flow, denies access to sensitive areas, and provides architectural features advantageous to reaction force personnel is effective in reducing the risk of an effective terrorist attack. In security circles, this concept is called CPTED (Crime Prevention Through Environmental Design – pronounced SEP-TED) and is based on Oscar Newman's book, <u>Creating Defensible Space</u>.

Chapter

5

Comparison To Other Risk Methodologies

Comparison Of Chemical Facility Vulnerability Assessment Methodologies

This chapter was written to provide the reader with a comparison between the RAMCAP methodologies required by the regulations specified by the Department of Homeland Security 6 CFR Part 27 and some of the more common methodologies that have been developed by other government agencies and industry. DHS has stipulated that they may approve methodologies in addition to the CSAT methodology either on an individual (facility) case basis or as an entire methodology, however the current regulations effectively "box" the facility into using the CSAT methodology for at least the SVA portion. Many of the readers of this book may have already completed a vulnerability assessment, and wish to know how to convert their existing information into the format required by the DHS regulations. By developing a "crosswalk" or "compliance matrix," this chapter is intended to show how each methodology meets or does not meet the requirements as set forth in the regulations. Note that although the

CSAT methodology states that it can be based either on assets or on scenarios, both the regulations and the methodology seem to lean heavily towards assets and so this chapter will also adopt that focus in the comparison of methodologies so that you will be able to capture the essence of the regulations.

From a practical perspective, a facility will most likely have only implemented one of the existing methodologies at their facility. To make it easier for a facility to compare their methodology with the CSAT methodology, each subsection describing the individual methodologies and comparing them to the CSAT methodology is designed to stand alone, so there may be some duplicate information provided in the following sections.

Sandia National Labs[21]

1. **Screening** – The Sandia process begins with a screening technique to determine which facilities are higher risk versus lower risk. Under the CSAT methodology, this task is completed by DHS as part of the "Top-Screen" process. Under the top-screen process, DHS will look at all facilities nationwide and place them in tiers to stipulate what risk-based standards they must meet. In other words, the chemical facility will not need to determine which facilities they will focus on, as DHS will tell them. It may still behoove a nationwide company with multiple facilities to perform some sort of a screening process if they wish to provide security above and beyond the performance standards as defined by DHS. The screening process may help the company decide which facilities to spend resources on first.

2. **Threat Assessment** – The Sandia document provides for three steps in determining what threats apply to the facility. First, threats are identified in a process of using open source (and if available, closed source) information to determine what types of

---

21 Vulnerability Assessment Methodology for Chemical Facilities (VAM-CF[SM]) USDOJ, 2002.

adversaries might attack the facility. These adversaries can range from vandals to armed terrorist groups. Once the adversaries are identified, in the second step, they are described in terms of equipment, vehicles, weapons and tactics. Finally, the team will assign a probability of attack to each adversary. Contrary to this approach, the CSAT methodology states that "You should assume that international terrorism is possible at any facility."

3. **Facility Characterization** – Characterizing the facility, in terms of the Sandia methodology, means describing the facility in terms of everything from operating procedures to process variables to recognizability and accessibility. The CSAT methodology describes this portion of the process as "asset characterization" and focuses on items, people, or information that an adversary could attack. Note that in the Sandia methodology, the characterization will focus much more on the facility as a whole, while in the CSAT methodology, you will be focusing specifically on the assets in the facility. If you have already performed your SVA using the Sandia National Labs' methodology, you will need to review your Facility Characterization to ensure that all of the assets described in the CSAT methodology were also characterized during the process. If they were, then you can document that the assets were characterized during that step. If they were not, then you will need to review all of your assets that were not characterized and determine what level of characterization they will need.

4. **Site Survey** – Both methodologies have a site survey step included as part of the information gathering portion of the process. The premise is that one cannot understand the ability of an adversary to cause harm without seeing first hand the site and possible attacks that can be made. There is a significant difference between the drawings on the Process and Instrumentation Diagrams or even the actual layout drawings and the equipment in the field. Keep in mind that when you are performing the site survey for the CSAT methodology, you are likely to be looking more at assets, and in the Sandia Methodology you will be focusing on possible scenarios.

5. **Determine Severity** – Both methodologies require the user to assign a qualitative severity to the scenario (in the case of Sandia) or damage to, theft of, or loss of the asset (in the case of CSAT.) These severities may be radically different, however. The Sandia severity scale recommends taking into account the severity scale from the Process Hazard Analysis, and the samples provided show high severities resulting from a single fatality or offsite release of chemical. The CSAT methodology provides sample severities ranging from 0-100 fatalities at the low end and 51,201-102,400 fatalities at the high end. Note that when developing a crosswalk to compare the results from these two methodologies, the severity scale will be one of the most difficult problems to resolve as most of the scenarios from the Sandia National Labs' methodology, will fall into the low end of the scale for the CSAT methodology.

6. **Determine Likelihood** – Each methodology asks the facility to define a likelihood for each event. (Note that, similar to the severities, these are qualitative. The facility does not have to be able to mathematically prove that there is an xx% chance of a terrorist attack.) In the Sandia National Labs' methodology, the likelihood is broken apart into two parts. First, the Likelihood of Attack (L_A) is determined based upon the threat assessment. This can be done using numerous methodologies (e.g.

CARVER, SHOCK, etc.) and can even be a relative likelihood. Usually, a team will assign the L_A for each of several possible adversaries. These Likelihoods of Attack are combined (using a matrix) with the Severity assigned to each scenario to determine the Likelihood of the Severity (L_S). A second likelihood value is assigned based upon the probability of a given adversary being able to successfully carry out their attack in spite of the existing safeguards. This value is called the Likelihood of Adversary Success. (L_{AS}) Contrary to this complex likelihood, the CSAT methodology has the facility assign a probability of success for the adversaries, but addresses the likelihood of an attack by stating that "...international terrorism is possible at every facility."

7. **Determine Risk** – Once the severities and likelihoods have been developed, both methodologies combine the values to develop a risk. The Sandia methodology uses a second matrix to combine the Likelihood of Adversary Success (L_{AS}) with the Likelihood of Severity (L_S) to determine the Risk (R) of the scenario. The matrix provided in the CSAT methodology combines Severity and Likelihood to assign a "High", "Medium" or "Low" risk to impacts on each asset. In order to convert Sandia risk values to CSAT risks, a facility may be able to develop a qualitative matrix which provides a direct correlation between the values.

8. **Make recommendations** – once the scenarios (assets) have been ranked according to risk, each methodology has the facility develop recommendations for improving their security. In the Sandia methodology, these recommendations may take the form of either preventing an event from occurring, or may mitigate the impacts of such an event if the adversary is successful in completing an attack.

9. **Final Report** – Both methodologies require the facility to develop a final report. The Sandia methodology suggests the

following items for inclusion in the final report:

1. Screening process results.
2. Facility characterization matrix and critical nodes analyzed.
3. Severity level definition table and severity level for each undesired event.
4. Threat definition table.
5. L_A (Likelihood of Attack) level definition table and L_A levels for each undesired event/adversary group.
6. L_S (Likelihood of Severity) priority ranking matrix and L_S levels for each undesired event/adversary group.
7. Priority undesired event/adversary groups analyzed.
8. Most vulnerable adversary scenarios for physical path for each priority undesired event/adversary group.
9. Most vulnerable adversary scenarios for process control path for each priority undesired event/adversary group.
10. L_{AS} (Likelihood of Adversary Success) level definition table for physical paths and L_{AS} levels for each priority undesired event/adversary group.
11. L_{AS} level definition table for process control paths and L_{AS} levels for each priority undesired event/adversary group.
12. Risk priority ranking matrix and risk levels for both physical paths and process control paths for each priority undesired event/adversary group (risk level summary table).
13. Summary of recommendations to reduce risk levels.

While the CSAT methodology does not specify the requirements in the final report, the SVA must be submitted to DHS per the schedule laid out in the regulations. Note that DHS will most likely want the final report of the SVA as opposed to the entire SVA with all of the supporting documentation, however the regulations do not stipulate how much information they will want in the SVA submission. The

recommendations (and existing countermeasures) should serve as the basis for the Site Security Plan.

American Petroleum Institute (API) Methodology[22]

1. **Screening** – Before the API SVA process is even started, the methodology requires the facility to screen issues based upon "asset attractiveness." Based upon consequence and target attractiveness, the facility will screen its assets for prioritization of analyses. API does state that consequence should be the dominant factor, but that the attractiveness of the target should also play a part.

Note that under the CSAT methodology, this task is completed by DHS as part of the "Top-Screen" process. Under the top-screen process, DHS will look at all facilities nationwide and place them in tiers to stipulate what risk-based standards they must meet. In other words, the chemical facility will not need to determine which facilities they will focus on, as DHS will tell them.

2. **Threat Assessment** – Step 2 of the API methodology is to complete an analysis of the threats that might potentially harm the facility, and includes the step of determining the target's

---

22 Security Vulnerability Assessment Methodology for the Petroleum and Petrochemical Industries, Second Edition October, 2004

attractiveness as a part of the threat assessment. While the process is not broken down into specific steps as in the Sandia methodology, API does call out internal, external and internally assisted threats, as well as both open and closed source information. Contrary to this approach, the CSAT methodology states that "You should assume that international terrorism is possible at any facility."

3. **Facility Characterization** – Step 1 of the API methodology is to conduct an asset characterization. This step and the preceding one can be completed in parallel, so the order will make no difference to the implementer. While the API methodology states that asset characterization focuses on petroleum or chemical processes, they do state that any asset may be considered. The CSAT methodology calls out several assets and states that they will be addressed as part of the study, so someone who is trying to draw the parallel between their existing API study and compliance with the new regulations will need to ensure that all of the assets were captured during the original study, or will need to update their study to include all of the assets as called out in the regulations. For each asset, both methodologies state that the following characterizing steps should be completed:
    1. Identify Critical Assets
    2. Identify Critical Functions
    3. Identify Critical Infrastructures and Dependencies
    4. Evaluate Existing Countermeasures
    5. Evaluate Impacts
    6. Select Targets for Further Analysis

4. **Site Survey** – the CSAT methodology calls out a requirement for the team to actually survey the site and look for places where an adversary can access the facility or cause damage. There is no comparable requirement in the API methodology. Note however, that it will be difficult to perform the steps laid out in the "Vulnerability Analysis" portion of the API study without

surveying the site. The API Vulnerability Analysis steps are:
1. Define Scenarios and Evaluate Specific Consequences
2. Evaluate Effectiveness of Existing Security Measures
3. Identify Vulnerabilities and Estimate Degree of Vulnerability

The facility that is trying to match their API SVA to the CSAT methodology will need to ensure that their Vulnerability Analysis included all of the steps required for the CSAT Site Survey and the team has visited the site to survey possible vulnerabilities.

5. **Determine Severity** – While API states that the facility needs to assign a severity based upon a conservative estimate of the expected consequences, the document does not include an explanation of which severity ranking should be assigned to a given level of consequence. The CSAT methodology has a provided sample matrix with severities ranging from 0-100 fatalities at the low end and 51,201-102,400 fatalities at the high end. Note that when developing a crosswalk to compare the results from these two methodologies, the severity scale will be one of the most difficult problems to resolve as most of the scenarios from the API methodology will most likely fall into the low end of the scale for the CSAT methodology.

6. **Determine Likelihood** – While the likelihood in the API methodology should be based upon the success of the entire scenario, the document does not explain which likelihood should be assigned to what probability of adversary success. The CSAT methodology has the team assign a probability of success for the adversaries, but addresses the likelihood of an attack by stating that "...international terrorism is possible at every facility."

7. **Determine Risk** – The API methodology provides a 5X5 risk matrix to determine risks to the facility and classify them as "High", "Medium", and "Low". This matrix is identical to the matrix provided in the CSAT methodology. As long as there is

sufficient correlation for the inputs (Severities and Likelihoods) to the Risk Ranking Matrix, the final results from an API study should be compatible with a CSAT study.

8. **Make recommendations** – The API methodology that includes a step for defining recommendations and prioritizing them for future action is identical to the comparable step from the CSAT methodology. The final results from an API study should be compatible with a CSAT study. The recommendations (and existing countermeasures) should serve as the basis for the Site Security Plan.

9. Final Report – both the API and CSAT methodologies stipulate a final report, but neither of them specifies the makeup and elements of the final report. The SVA must be submitted to DHS per the schedule laid out in the regulations. Note that DHS will most likely want the final report of the SVA as opposed to the entire SVA with all of the supporting documentation, however the regulations do not stipulate how much information they will want in the SVA submission.

Guidelines for Analyzing and Managing the Security Vulnerabilities of Fixed Chemical Sites

Center For Chemical Process Safety (CCPS) Methodology[23]

1. **Screening** – The CCPS methodology has an *optional* first step of screening the

23 Guidelines for Analyzing and Managing the Security Vulnerabilities of Fixed Chemical Sites AIChE, 2003.

facilities to prioritize hazards across all of a company's facilities. This "Enterprise Level Screening" is similar to those in the Sandia and API methodologies, but as before, is not a part of the CSAT methodology, since this task is completed by DHS as part of the "Top-Screen" process. Under the top-screen process, DHS will look at all facilities nationwide and place them in tiers to stipulate what risk-based standards they must meet. In other words, the chemical facility will not need to determine which facilities they will focus on, as DHS will tell them. If a company does wish to prioritize their facilities across the entire enterprise, Appendix B of the CCPS Book includes a methodology for screening facilities. While the process cannot be used in place of the Top-Screen process required by DHS, it can be used to supplement the DHS process, and allow facilities to prioritize the order of implementation for their recommendations across all facilities.

1. The first step in the CCPS methodology is actually Project Planning which has no formal counterpart in the CSAT methodology. However, it will be impossible to comply with all of the legal requirements of the DHS regulations without properly planning the project. If the facility has developed their Project Plan in accordance with the plan mentioned in Chapter 3 of <u>Keeping Our Chemical Facilities Safe</u>, then they will most likely have complied with the requirements of the CCPS methodology and vice versa.

2. **Facility Characterization** – The second step in the CCPS methodology is facility characterization. Similar to the methodologies mentioned above, the intention is to identify and characterize the specifics of the assets which the company is trying to protect. The CCPS methodology states that asset characterization focuses on "...highly hazardous chemicals and key assets, with an emphasis on possible public impacts.[24]" The

---

24   <u>Guidelines for Analyzing and Managing the Security Vulnerabilities of Fixed Chemical Sites</u>. p 49

CSAT methodology has an example list of several assets but someone who is trying to draw the parallel between their existing CCPS study and compliance with the new regulations will need to ensure that all of the assets required to be addressed in CSAT were captured during the original CCPS study, or will need to update their study to include all of the assets as called out in the regulations. There is a slight difference between the six steps called out in the CCPS methodology and the CSAT methodology. For each asset, both methodologies state that the following characterizing steps should be completed:

CSAT Steps	CCPS Steps
1. Identify Critical Asset	1. Critical Assets Identification
2. Identify Critical Functions	2. Hazards Identification
3. Identify Critical Infrastructures and Dependencies	3. Consequence Analysis
4. Evaluate Existing Countermeasures	4. Attractiveness Analysis
5. Evaluate Impacts	5. Layers of Protection Review
6. Select Targets for Further Analysis	6. Potential Target List

Note that these steps do not match up directly, so you may have a difficult time drawing your compliance matrix from one to the other in order to demonstrate that you have completed the CSAT requirements. Note also that many of the CCPS steps seem to fit better in the Vulnerability Assessment phase as part of a scenario development, rather than as part of the facility characterization.

3. **Threat Assessment** – The fourth step in the CCPS methodology consists of a threat assessment. There are two

steps in the CCPS threat assessment: Adversary Identification and Adversary Characterization. In other words, "figure out who might want to hurt the facility and then figure out what their approach will be." Appendix C of the CCPS book provides a Threat Assessment Worksheet for a facility to use when developing their Threat Assessment. Contrary to this approach, the CSAT methodology states that "You should assume that international terrorism is possible at any facility."

4. **Site Survey** – There is no requirement in the CCPS methodology to perform an actual walkdown of the facility. The CCPS methodology states that the people facilitating the discussion need to be those "...most familiar with the facility." While this statement does not conflict with the CSAT methodology, and should meet the requirements of the regulations, it is our belief that the person facilitating the discussion should be the person most familiar with the methodology being used, as they will know what questions to ask of **all** of the team members to get the best analysis of the vulnerabilities and recommendations.

   Step 4 of the CCPS methodology is the Vulnerability Assessment itself and the book details both an asset-based and scenario-based approach. The asset-based approach focuses only on assets that have significant consequences. The scenario-based approach begins the same way that the asset-based approach does, but analyzes each scenario in more depth to draw out scenarios that might not be sufficiently detailed in the asset-based analysis. While a facility may save money by only analyzing the high-profile assets, note that with DHS' definition of "asset," it may be difficult to ensure that no "high-profile" assets are missed.

5. **Determine Severity** – The severity is determined in step 3 of the CCPS methodology, but essentially, the only real difference from the CSAT methodology is that the examples provided by

each methodology are different.

6. **Determine Likelihood** – The likelihood is determined in step 3 of the CCPS methodology, but essentially, the only real difference from the CSAT methodology is that the examples provided by each methodology are different.

7. **Determine Risk** – The risk is determined in step 3 of the CCPS methodology, but essentially, the only real difference from the CSAT methodology is that the examples provided by each methodology are different.

8. **Make Recommendations** – Recommendations are developed in Step 5 of the CCPS methodology. The major difference between the two methodologies is that the CCPS methodology instructs the team to determine the new risk value after the recommendation has been implemented in order to prioritize implementation of the recommendations.

9. **Final Report** – The CCPS methodology does not have a formal section on developing a final report.

10. Integration – The CCPS methodology has a section on integrating a facility's SVA with their existing programs. As mentioned before, if a facility has done so, then they will need to ensure that they understand the ramifications of the parts of the program that need to be classified as CVI and the facility will need to go over their existing SVA information and label all of the information that needs to be labeled as CVI.

Chapter

6

Summary/Conclusion

The process of determining a chemical facility's vulnerabilities to terrorist attack is relatively simple, perhaps deceptively so. Process engineers and process operators are very knowledgeable about the parameters of the process units they oversee. They have an in-depth understanding of how the different chemicals and mixtures in their units are supposed to behave. They have the ability to tell when their unit is "acting up", and can quickly take steps to control the reactions in their units to prevent any operations outside of the set parameters of that unit. They can draw upon historical data to learn from past issues involving their unit, as well as the corrective techniques used by previous stewards of the unit in question.

"Simple" however, does not mean "easy." Unfortunately, the intricate process of operating and monitoring that unit does not address the many threats posed against a facility by deliberate attacks. An operator may have a complete understanding of the issues surrounding a storage vessel in his unit, but may not even consider the consequences of a rocket propelled grenade slamming into that same storage vessel. Operators tend to look within the confines of the units for which they are responsible; an outsider's point of view may be required to present the list of concerns from external attack.

Contrariwise, an outside security expert rarely understands the chemical process or the true consequences of an adverse event.

They may not understand the internal or external politics with which the company has to live every day. If their background is from government, they may not truly understand the budget limitations under which the facility must operate. If they are from private security, then they may not have the understanding of the threat or know what modes of attack a terrorist organization might attempt.

No single individual will have all of the expertise to provide

a facility with a comprehensive Security Vulnerability Assessment unless they are working for the terrorists themselves. On the other hand, the facility must comply with the regulations DHS has published to enter their data in the Top-Screen process, perform a Security Vulnerability Assessment, and develop a Site Security Plan. The process is complicated, but not impossible. While we can't give you the knowledge and skills to complete every part of the regulations by yourself, this book is an introduction to each phase of the process, and will hopefully allow you to have the insight necessary to bring the required skills together and comply with the regulations.

This book is designed provide insight into the methodology chemical facilities must use to determine their levels of vulnerability to terrorist attack. This book will contribute to the education required to counter the threats of those who would do this nation harm. All those those involved in vulnerability assessments should "think outside of the box," and resist the pre-9/11 dismissive attitude when considering threats to a facility posed by terrorists. Even if a given scenario seems impossible, the Study Team needs to address it, so that it will have at least been discussed. Keep an open mind, and the team will come up with the best possible study that their skills and talents can produce.

> *"We have to be lucky every time to succeed. The terrorists only have to get lucky once."*
> – **Deputy Attorney General Larry D. Thompson**

Appendix

Chemicals of Interest (From Final Interim Regulations – to be updated by DHS)

Chemical of Interest	Chemical Abstract Service (CAS) Number	Screening Threshold Quantity (STQ) (lbs)
1,1,3,3,3-pentafluoro-2-(trifluoromethyl)-1-propene	382-21-8	Any Amount
1,1-Dimethylhydrazine	57-14-7	11,250
1,2-bis(2-chloroethylthio)ethane	3563-36-8	Any Amount
1,3-bis(2-chloroethylthio)-n-propane	63905-10-2	Any Amount
1,3-Butadiene	106-99-0	7,500
1,3-Pentadiene	504-60-9	7,500
1,4-bis(2-chloroethylthio)-n-butane	142868-93-7	Any Amount

Chemical of Interest	Chemical Abstract Service (CAS) Number	Screening Threshold Quantity (STQ) (lbs)
1,5-bis(2-chloroethylthio)-n-pentane	142868-94-8	Any Amount
1-Butene	106-98-9	7,500
1-Chloropropylene	590-21-6	7,500
1H-Tetrazole	16681-77-9	2,000
1-Pentane	109-67-1	7,500
2,2-Dimethylpropane	463-82-1	7,500
2-Butene	107-01-7	7,500
2-Butene-cis	590-18-1	7,500
2-Butene-trans	624-64-6	7,500
2-chloroethylchloromethylsulfide	2625-76-5	Any Amount
2-Chloropropylene	557-98-2	7,500
2-Chlorovinyldichloroarsine	541-25-3	Any Amount
2-Methyl-1-butene	563-46-2	7,500
2-Methylpropene	115-11-7	7,500
2-Pentene, (Z)-	627-20-3	7,500
2-Pentene,(E)-	646-04-8	7,500
3,3-dimethyl-2-butanol	464-07-3	Any Amount
3-Methyl-1-butene	563-45-1	7,500
3-Quinuclidinyl benzilate (BZ)	62869-69-6	Any Amount
5-Nitrobenzotriazol	2338-12-7	2,000

Chemical of Interest	Chemical Abstract Service (CAS) Number	Screening Threshold Quantity (STQ) (lbs)
Acetaldehyde	75-07-0	7,500
Acetone	67-64-1	2,000
Acetone cyanohydrin, stabilized	75-86-5	2,000
Acetyl bromide	506-96-7	2,000
Acetyl chloride	75-36-5	2,000
Acetyl iodide	507-02-8	2,000
Acetylene	74-86-2	7,500
Acrolein	107-02-8	3,750
Acrylonitrile	107-13-1	15,000
Acrylyl chloride	814-68-6	3,750
Allyl alcohol	107-18-6	11,250
Allylamine	107-11-9	7,500
Allyltrichlorosilane, stabilized	107-37-9	2,000
Aluminum bromide, anhydrous	7727-15-3	2,000
Aluminum chloride, anhydrous	7446-70-0	2,000
Aluminum phosphide	20859-73-8	2,000
Ammonia (anhydrous)	7664-41-7	7,500
Ammonia (conc. 20% or greater)	7664-41-7	15,000
Ammonium nitrate (nitrogen concentration of 28%34%)	6484-52-2	2,000
Ammonium perchlorate	7790-98-9	2,000
Ammonium picrate	131-74-8	2,000
Amyltrichlorosilane	107-72-2	2,000
Antimony pentafluoride	7783-70-2	2,000

Chemical of Interest	Chemical Abstract Service (CAS) Number	Screening Threshold Quantity (STQ) (lbs)
Arsenous trichloride	7784-34-1	Any Amount
Arsine	7784-42-1	Any Amount
Barium azide	18810-58-7	2,000
bis(2-chloroethyl)ethylamine	538-07-8	Any Amount
bis(2-chloroethyl)methylamine	51-75-2	Any Amount
bis(2-chloroethyl)sulfide	505-60-2	Any Amount
bis(2-chloroethylthio)methane	63869-13-6	Any Amount
bis(2-chloroethylthioethyl)ether	63918-89-8	Any Amount
bis(2-chloroethylthiomethyl)ether	63918-90-1	Any Amount
bis(2-chlorovinyl)chloroarsine	40334-69-8	Any Amount
Boron tribromide	10294-33-4	2,000
Boron trichloride	10294-34-5	Any Amount
Boron triflouride	7637-07-2	Any Amount
Boron triflouride compound with methyl ether (1:1)	353-42-4	11,250
Bromine	7726-95-6	7,500

Chemical of Interest	Chemical Abstract Service (CAS) Number	Screening Threshold Quantity (STQ) (lbs)
Bromine chloride	13863-41-7	Any Amount
Bromine pentafluoride	7789-30-2	2,000
Bromine trifluoride	7787-71-5	2,000
Bromotrifluorethylene	598-73-2	7,500
Butane	106-97-8	7,500
Butene	25167-67-3	7,500
Butyltrichlorosilane	7521-80-4	2,000
Calcium dithionite	15512-36-4	2,000
Calcium hydrosulfite	15512-36-4	2,000
Calcium phosphide	1305-99-3	2,000
Carbon disulfide	75-15-0	15,000
Carbon monoxide	630-08-0	Any Amount
Carbon oxysulfide	463-58-1	7,500
Carbonyl fluoride	353-50-4	Any Amount
Carbonyl sulfide	463-58-1	Any Amount
Chlorine	7782-50-5	1,875
Chlorine dioxide	10049-04-4	2,000
Chlorine monoxide	7791-21-1	7,500
Chlorine pentafluoride	13637-63-3	Any Amount

Chemical of Interest	Chemical Abstract Service (CAS) Number	Screening Threshold Quantity (STQ) (lbs)
Chlorine trifluoride	7790-91-2	Any Amount
Chloroacetyl chloride	79-04-9	2,000
Chloroform	67-66-3	15,000
Chloromethyl ether	542-88-1	750
Chloromethyl methyl ether	107-30-2	3,750
Chloropicrin	76-06-2	Any Amount
Chlorosulfonic acid	7790-94-5	2,000
Chromium oxychloride	7803-51-2	2,000
Crotonaldehyde	4170-30-3	15,000
Crotonaldehyde, (E)-	123-73-9	15,000
Cyanogen	460-19-5	Any Amount
Cyanogen chloride	506-77-4	Any Amount
Cyclohexylamine	108-91-8	11,250
Cyclohexyltrichlorosilane	98-12-4	2,000
Cyclopropane	75-19-4	7,500
Cyclotetramethylenetetranitramine	2691-41-0	2,000
Diazodinitrophenol	87-31-0	2,000
Diborane	19287-45-7	Any Amount
Dichlorosilane	4109-96-0	Any Amount

Chemical of Interest	Chemical Abstract Service (CAS) Number	Screening Threshold Quantity (STQ) (lbs)
Diethyl ethylphosphonate	78-38-6	Any Amount
Diethyl N,N-dimethylphosphoramidate	2404-03-7	Any Amount
Diethyl phosphate	762-04-9	Any Amount
Diethyldichlorosilane	1719-53-5	2,000
Diethyleneglycol dinitrate,	693-21-0	2,000
Difluoroethane	75-37-6	7,500
Dimethyl ethylphosphonate	6163-75-3	Any Amount
Dimethyl methylphosphonate	756-79-6	Any Amount
Dimethyl phosphate	868-85-9	Any Amount
Dimethylamine	124-40-3	7,500
Dimethyldichlorosilane	75-78-5	2,000
Dimethylphosphoramidodichloridate	677-43-0	Any Amount
Dinitrogen tetroxide	10544-72-6	Any Amount
Dinitroglycoluril	55510-04-8	2,000
Dinitrophenol	25550-58-7	2,000
Dinitroresorcinol	35860-51-6	2,000
Dinitrosobenzene	25550-55-4	2,000

Chemical of Interest	Chemical Abstract Service (CAS) Number	Screening Threshold Quantity (STQ) (lbs)
Diphenyl-2-hydroxyacetic acid (aka benzilic acid)	76-93-7	Any Amount
Diphenyldichlorosilane	80-10-4	2,000
Dipicryl sulfide	2217-06-3	2,000
Dodecyltrichlorosilane	4484-72-4	2,000
Epichlorohydrin	106-89-8	15,000
Ethane	74-84-0	7,500
Ethyl acetylene	107-00-6	7,500
Ethyl chloride	75-00-3	7,500
Ethyl ether	60-29-7	7,500
Ethyl mercaptan	75-08-1	7,500
Ethyl nitrite	109-95-5	7,500
Ethyl phosphonyl dichloride	1066-50-8	Any Amount
Ethyl phosphonyl difluoride	753-98-0	Any Amount
Ethylamine	75-04-7	7,500
Ethyldiethanolamine	139-87-7	Any Amount
Ethylene	74-85-1	7,500
Ethylene oxide	75-21-8	Any Amount
Ethylenediamine	107-15-3	15,000
Ethyleneimine	151-56-4	7,500
Ethyltrichlorosilane	115-21-9	2,000

Chemical of Interest	Chemical Abstract Service (CAS) Number	Screening Threshold Quantity (STQ) (lbs)
Fluorine	7782-41-4	Any Amount
Fluorosulfonic acid	7789-21-1	2,000
Formaldehyde (solution)	50-00-0	11,250
Furan	110-00-9	3,750
Germane	7782-65-2	Any Amount
Germanium tetrafluoride	7783-58-6	Any Amount
Guanyl nitrosaminoguanylidene hydrazine		2,000
Guanyl nitrosaminoguanyltetrazene	109-27-3	2,000
Hexaethyl tetraphosphate and compressed gas mixtures	757-58-4	Any Amount
Hexafluoroacetone	684-16-2	Any Amount
Hexanitrodiphenylamine	35860-31-2	2,000
Hexanitrostilbene	20062-22-0	2,000
Hexolite	121-82-4	2,000
Hexotonal	107-15-3	2,000
Hexyltrichlorosilane	928-89-2 6	2,000
Hydrazine	302-01-2	11,250
Hydrochloric acid (conc. 37% or greater)	7647-01-0	11,250
Hydrocyanic acid	74-90-8	1,875
Hydrogen	1333-74-0	7,500

Chemical of Interest	Chemical Abstract Service (CAS) Number	Screening Threshold Quantity (STQ) (lbs)
Hydrogen bromide, anhydrous	10035-10-6	Any Amount
Hydrogen chloride (anhydrous)	7647-01-0	Any Amount
Hydrogen cyanide	74-90-8	Any Amount
Hydrogen fluoride/Hydrofluoric acid (conc. 50% or greater)	7664-39-3	750
Hydrogen iodide, anhydrous	10034-85-2	Any Amount
Hydrogen peroxide (concentration of at least 30%)	7722-84-1	2,000
Hydrogen selenide	7783-07-5	Any Amount
Hydrogen sulfide	7783-06-4	Any Amount
Iodine pentafluoride	7783-66-6	2,000
Iron, pentacarbonyl-	13463-40-6	1,875
Isobutane	75-28-5	7,500
Isobutyronitrile	78-82-0	15,000
Isopentane	78-78-4	7,500
Isoprene	78-79-5	7,500
Isopropyl chloride	75-29-6	7,500
Isopropyl chloroformate	108-23-6	11,250
Isopropylamine	75-31-0	7,500
Lead azide	13424-46-9	2,000

Chemical of Interest	Chemical Abstract Service (CAS) Number	Screening Threshold Quantity (STQ) (lbs)
Lead styphnate	15245-44-0	2,000
Lithium amide	7782-89-0	2,000
Lithium nitride	26134-62-3	2,000
Magnesium aluminum phosphide		2,000
Magnesium diamide	7803-54-5	2,000
Magnesium phosphide	12057-74-8	2,000
Mannitol hexanitrate, wetted	15825-70-4	2,000
Mercury fulminate	628-86-4	2,000
Methacrylonitrile	126-98-7	7,500
Methane	74-82-8	7,500
Methyl bromide	74-83-9	Any Amount
Methyl chloride	74-87-3	7,500
Methyl chloroformate	79-22-1	3,750
Methyl ether	115-10-6	7,500
Methyl formate	107-31-3	7,500
Methyl hydrazine	60-34-4	11,250
Methyl isocyanate	624-83-9	11,250
Methyl mercaptan	74-93-1	Any Amount
Methyl phosphonyl dichloride	676-97-1	Any Amount
Methyl phosphonyl difluoride	676-99-3	Any Amount
Methyl thiocyanate	556-64-9	15,000

Chemical of Interest	Chemical Abstract Service (CAS) Number	Screening Threshold Quantity (STQ) (lbs)
Methylamine	74-89-5	7,500
Methylchlorosilane	993-00-0	Any Amount
Methyldichlorosilane	75-54-7	2,000
Methyldiethanolamine	105-59-9	Any Amount
Methylphenyldichlorosilane	149-74-6	2,000
Methyltrichlorosilane	75-79-6	2,000
N,N-diisopropyl-2-aminoethyl chloride hydrochloride	4261-68-1	Any Amount
N,N-diisopropyl-β-aminoethanol	96-80-0	Any Amount
N,N-diisopropyl-β-aminoethyl chloride	96-79-7	Any Amount
Nickel Carbonyl	13463-39-3	750
Nitric acid	7697-37-2	2,000
Nitric oxide	10102-43-9	Any Amount
Nitro urea	556-89-8	2,000
Nitrocellulose	9004-70-0	2,000
Nitrogen trioxide	10544-73-7	Any Amount
Nitroglycerine	55-63-0	2,000
Nitroguanidine	556-88-7	2,000
Nitromethane	75-52-5	2,000
Nitrostarch	9056-38-6	2,000

Chemical of Interest	Chemical Abstract Service (CAS) Number	Screening Threshold Quantity (STQ) (lbs)
Nitrosyl chloride	2696-92-6	Any Amount
Nitrotriazolone	932-64-9	2,000
Nonyltrichlorosilane	5283-67-0	2,000
o,o-diethyl S-[2-(diethylamino)ethyl] phosphorothiolate	78-53-5	Any Amount
Octadecyltrichlorosilane	112-04-9	2,000
Octolite	68610-51-5	2,000
Octonal	124-13-0	2,000
Octyltrichlorosilane	5283-66-9	2,000
o-ethyl-N,N-dimethylphosphoramido-cyanidate	77-81-6	Any Amount
o-ethyl-o-2-diisopropylaminoethyl methylphosphonite	57856-11-8	Any Amount
o-ethyl-S-2-diisopropylaminoethyl methyl phosphonothiolate	50782-69-9	Any Amount
o-isopropyl methylphosphonochloridate	1445-76-7	Any Amount
o-isopropyl methylphosphonofluoridate	107-44-8	Any Amount
Oleum (Fuming Sulfuric acid)	8014-95-7	7,500
o-pinacolyl methylphosphonochloridate	7040-57-5	Any Amount
o-pinacolyl methylphosphonofluoridate	96-64-0	Any Amount
Oxygen difluoride	7783-41-7	Any Amount

119

Chemical of Interest	Chemical Abstract Service (CAS) Number	Screening Threshold Quantity (STQ) (lbs)
Pentaerythrite tetranitrate or PETN	78-11-5	2,000
Pentane	109-66-0	7,500
Pentolite	8066-33-9	2,000
Peracetic acid	79-21-0	7,500
Perchloromethylmercaptan	594-42-3	7,500
Perchloryl fluoride	7616-94-6	Any Amount
Phenyltrichlorosilane	98-13-5	2,000
Phosgene	75-44-5	Any Amount
Phosphine	7803-51-2	Any Amount
Phosphorus	7723-14-0	Any Amount
Phosphorus oxychloride	10025-87-3	Any Amount
Phosphorus oxychloride	10025-87-3	2,000
Phosphorus pentachloride	10026-13-8	Any Amount
Phosphorus pentachloride	10026-13-8	2,000
Phosphorus pentasulfide	1314-80-3	2,000
Phosphorus trichloride	7719-12-2	Any Amount
Phosphorus trichloride	7719-12-2	2,000
Piperidine	110-89-4	11,250
Potassium chlorate	3811-04-9	2,000

Chemical of Interest	Chemical Abstract Service (CAS) Number	Screening Threshold Quantity (STQ) (lbs)
Potassium cyanide	151-50-8	2,000
Potassium nitrate	7757-79-1	2,000
Potassium perchlorate	7778-74-7	2,000
Potassium phosphide	20770-41-6	2,000
Propadiene	463-49-0	7,500
Propane	74-98-6	7,500
Propionitrile	107-12-0	7,500
Propyl chlorofromate	109-61-5	11,250
Propylene	115-07-1	7,500
Propylene oxide	75-56-9	7,500
Propyleneimine	75-55-8	7,500
Propyltrichlorosilane	141-57-1	2,000
Propyne	74-99-7	7,500
Quinuclidine-3-ol	1619-34-7	Any Amount
RDX and HMX mixtures	121-82-4	2,000
Selenium hexafluoride	7783-79-1	Any Amount
Silane	7803-62-5	7,500
Silicon tetrachloride	10026-04-7	2,000
Silicon tetrafluoride	7783-61-1	Any Amount
Sodium chlorate	7775-09-9	2,000
Sodium cyanide	143-33-9	2,000

Chemical of Interest	Chemical Abstract Service (CAS) Number	Screening Threshold Quantity (STQ) (lbs)
Sodium dinitro-o-cresolate	25641-53-6	2,000
Sodium dithionite	7775-14-6	2,000
Sodium hydrosulfite	7775-14-6	2,000
Sodium nitrate	7631-99-4	2,000
Sodium phosphide	7558-80-7	2,000
Sodium picramate	831-52-7	2,000
Stibine	7803-52-3	Any Amount
Strontium phosphide	13450-99-2	2,000
Sulfur dichloride	10545-99-0	Any Amount
Sulfur dioxide (anhydrous)	7446-09-5	Any Amount
Sulfur monochloride	10025-67-9	Any Amount
Sulfur tetraflouride	7783-60-0	Any Amount
Sulfur trioxide	7446-11-9	7,500
Sulfuryl chloride	7791-25-5	2,000
Sulfuryl fluoride	2699-79-8	Any Amount
Tellurium hexafluoride	7783-80-4	Any Amount
Tetrafluoroethylene	116-14-3	7,500
Tetramethyllead	75-74-1	7,500
Tetramethylsilane	75-76-3	7,500

Chemical of Interest	Chemical Abstract Service (CAS) Number	Screening Threshold Quantity (STQ) (lbs)
Tetranitroaniline	53014-37-2	2,000
Tetranitromethane	509-14-8	7,500
Tetrazol-1-acetic acid	21732-17-2	2,000
Thiodiglycol	111-48-8	Any Amount
Thionyl chloride	7719-09-7	Any Amount
Thionyl chloride	7719-09-7	2,000
Titanium tetrachloride	7550-45-0	2,000
Toluene 2,4-diisocyanate	584-84-9	7,500
Toluene 2,6-diisocyanate	91-08-7	7,500
Toluene diisocyanate (unspecified isomer)	26471-62-5	7,500
Trichlorosilane	10025-78-2	2,000
Triethanolamine	102-71-6	Any Amount
Triethanolamine hydrochloride	637-39-8	Any Amount
Triethyl phosphite	122-52-1	Any Amount
Trifluoroacetyl chloride	354-32-5	Any Amount
Trifluorochloroethylene	79-38-9	Any Amount
Trimethyl phosphite	121-45-9	Any Amount

Chemical of Interest	Chemical Abstract Service (CAS) Number	Screening Threshold Quantity (STQ) (lbs)
Trimethylamine	75-50-3	Any Amount
Trimethylchlorosilane	75-77-4	2,000
Trinitroaniline	26952-42-1	2,000
Trinitroanisole	606-35-9	2,000
Trinitrobenzene	99-35-4	2,000
Trinitrobenzenesulfonic acid	2508-19-2	2,000
Trinitrobenzoic acid	129-66-8	2,000
Trinitrochlorobenzene	88-88-0	2,000
Trinitrofluorenone	129-79-3	2,000
Trinitro-meta-cresol	602-99-3	2,000
Trinitronaphthalene	558101-17-8	2,000
Trinitrophenetole	4732-14-3	2,000
Trinitrophenol	88-89-1	2,000
Trinitroresorcinol	82-71-3	2,000
Trinitrotoluene	118-96-7	2,000
Tris(2-chloroethyl)amine	555-77-1	Any Amount
Tris(2-chlorovinyl)arsine	40334-70-1	Any Amount
Tritonal	54413-15-9	2,000
Tungsten hexafluoride	7783-82-6	Any Amount
Uranium hexafluoride	7783-81-5	2,000
Urea	57-13-6	2,000

Chemical of Interest	Chemical Abstract Service (CAS) Number	Screening Threshold Quantity (STQ) (lbs)
Urea nitrate	124-47-0	2,000
Vinyl acetate monomer	108-05-4	11,250
Vinyl actylene	689-97-4	7,500
Vinyl chloride	75-01-4	7,500
Vinyl ethyl ether	109-92-2	7,500
Vinyl fluoride	75-02-5	7,500
Vinyl methyl ether	107-25-5	7,500
Vinylidene chloride	75-35-4	7,500
Vinylidene fluoride	75-38-7	7,500
Vinyltrichlorosilane	75-94-5	2,000
Zinc dithionite	7779-86-4	2,000
Zinc hydrosulfite	7779-86-4	2,000
Zirconium picramate	63868-82-6	2,000

Appendix

B

Regulations

This Appendix contains the text of the regulations with which facilities will have to comply and is provided for ease of reference to the reader. The only portions of the regulatory text that are included here are the actual items with prescriptive language. This Appendix does not include the first part of the regulations with the responses to comments from the Initial Proposed Regulations. For that text, refer to the full text of the regulations which can be located here:
http://a257.g.akamaitech.net/7/257/2422/01jan20071800/ edocket.access.gpo.gov/2007/E7-6363.htm

Part III
Department of Homeland Security
6 CFR Part 27
Chemical Facility Anti-Terrorism Standards; Final Rule

DEPARTMENT OF HOMELAND SECURITY
ACTION: Interim final rule.

SUMMARY: The Department of Homeland Security (DHS or Department) issues this interim final rule (IFR) pursuant to Section 550 of the Homeland Security Appropriations Act of 2007 (Section 550), which provided the Department with authority to promulgate ``interim final regulations'' for the security of certain chemical

facilities in the United States.

This rule establishes risk-based performance standards for the security of our Nation's chemical facilities. It requires covered chemical facilities to prepare Security Vulnerability Assessments (SVAs), which identify facility security vulnerabilities, and to develop and implement Site Security Plans (SSPs), which include measures that satisfy the identified risk-based performance standards. It also allows certain covered chemical facilities, in specified circumstances, to submit Alternate Security Programs (ASPs) in lieu of an SVA, SSP, or both.

The rule contains associated provisions addressing inspections and audits, recordkeeping, and the protection of information that constitutes Chemical-terrorism Vulnerability Information (CVI). Finally, the rule provides the Department with authority to seek compliance through the issuance of Orders, including Orders Assessing Civil Penalty and Orders for the Cessation of Operations.

EFFECTIVE DATES: This regulation is effective June 8, 2007, except for Appendix A to part 27. A subsequent final rule document will announce the effective date of Appendix A to Part 27. Comments related to the addition of Appendix A to part 27 only will be accepted until May 9, 2007.

ADDRESSES: You may submit comments, identified by docket number 2006-0073, by one of the following methods: Federal eRulemaking Portal: http://www.regulations.gov.

Follow the instructions for submitting comments. Mail: IP/CSCD/Dennis Deziel, Mail Stop 8100, Department of Homeland Security, Washington, DC 20528-8100.

FOR FURTHER INFORMATION CONTACT: Dennis Deziel, Chemical Security Regulatory Task Force, Department of Homeland Security, 703-235-5263.

SUPPLEMENTARY INFORMATION: This interim final rule is

organized as follows: Section I explains the public participation provisions and provides a brief discussion of the statutory and regulatory authority and history; Section II summarizes the changes from the Advance Notice
of Rulemaking and discusses the revised rule text; Section III summarizes and responds to the comments the Department received in response to the Advance Notice of Rulemaking; and Section IV contains the regulatory analyses for this interim final rule.

List of Subjects in 6 CFR Part 27

Chemical security, Facilities, Reporting and recordkeeping, Security measures.

The Interim Final Rule

For the reasons set forth in the preamble, the Department of Homeland Security adds Part 27 to Title 6, Code of Federal Regulations, to read as follows:

Title 6--Department of Homeland Security
Chapter 1--Department of Homeland Security, Office of the Secretary
PART 27--CHEMICAL FACILITY ANTI-TERRORISM STANDARDS

Subpart A--General
     Sec.   27.100 Purpose.
             27.105 Definitions.
             27.110 Applicability.
             27.115 Implementation.
             27.120 Designation of a coordinating official; Consultations and technical assistance.
             27.125 Severability.
Subpart B--Chemical Facility Security Program
             27.200 Information regarding security risk for a

chemical facility.

Authority: Pub. L. 109-295, sec. 550.

Subpart A--General

Sec. 27.100 Purpose.

The purpose of this Part is to enhance the security of our Nation by furthering the mission of the Department as provided in 6 U.S.C. ec. 111(b)(1) and by lowering the risk posed by certain chemical facilities.

Sec. 27.105 Definitions.

As used in this part:

Alternative Security Program or ASP shall mean a third-party or industry organization program, a local authority, state or Federal government program or any element or aspect thereof, that the Assistant Secretary has determined meets the requirements of this Part and provides for an equivalent level of security to that established by this Part.

Assistant Secretary shall mean the Assistant Secretary for Infrastructure Protection, Department of Homeland Security or his designee.

Chemical Facility or **facility** shall mean any establishment that possesses or plans to possess, at any relevant point in time, a quantity of a chemical substance determined by the Secretary to be potentially dangerous or that meets other risk-related criteria identified by the Department. As used herein, the term chemical facility or facility shall also refer to the owner or operator of the chemical facility. Where multiple owners and/or operators function within a common infrastructure or within a single fenced area, the Assistant Secretary may determine that such owners and/or operators constitute a single chemical facility or multiple chemical facilities depending on the circumstances.

Chemical Security Assessment Tool or CSAT shall mean a suite of four applications, including User Registration, Top-Screen, Security Vulnerability Assessment, and Site Security Plan, through which the Department will collect and analyze key data from

chemical facilities.

Chemical-terrorism Vulnerability Information or **CVI** shall mean the information listed in Sec. 27.400(b).

Coordinating Official shall mean the person (or his designee(s)) selected by the Assistant Secretary to ensure that the regulations are implemented in a uniform, impartial, and fair manner.

Covered Facility or **Covered Chemical Facility** shall mean a chemical facility determined by the Assistant Secretary to present high levels of security risk, or a facility that the Assistant Secretary has determined is presumptively high risk under Sec. 27.200.

Department shall mean the Department of Homeland Security.

Deputy Secretary shall mean the Deputy Secretary of the Department of Homeland Security or his designee.

Director of the Chemical Security Division or **Director** shall mean the Director of the Chemical Security Division, Office of Infrastructure Protection, Department of Homeland Security or any successors to that position within the Department or his designee.

General Counsel shall mean the General Counsel of the Department of Homeland Security or his designee.

Operator shall mean a person who has responsibility for the daily operations of a facility or facilities subject to this Part.

Owner shall mean the person or entity that owns any facility subject to this Part.

Present high levels of security risk and **high risk** shall refer to a chemical facility that, in the discretion of the Secretary of Homeland Security, presents a high risk of significant adverse consequences for human life or health, national security and/or critical economic assets if subjected to terrorist attack, compromise, infiltration, or exploitation.

Risk profiles shall mean criteria identified by the Assistant Secretary for determining which chemical facilities will complete the Top-Screen or provide other risk assessment information.

Screening Threshold Quantity or **STQ** shall mean the quantity of a chemical of interest, upon which the facility's obligation to complete and submit the CSAT Top-Screen is based.

Secretary or **Secretary of Homeland Security** shall mean the

Secretary of the Department of Homeland Security or any person, officer or entity within the Department to whom the Secretary's authority under Section 550 is delegated.

Terrorist attack or **terrorist incident** shall mean any incident or attempt that constitutes terrorism or terrorist activity under 6 U.S.C. 101(15) or 18 U.S.C. 2331(5) or 8 U.S.C. 1182(a)(3)(B)(iii), including any incident or attempt that involves or would involve sabotage of chemical facilities or theft, misappropriation or misuse of a dangerous quantity of chemicals.

Tier shall mean the risk level associated with a covered chemical facility and which is assigned to a facility by the Department. For purposes of this part, there are four risk-based tiers, ranging from highest risk at Tier 1 to lowest risk at Tier 4.

Top-Screen shall mean an initial screening process designed by the Assistant Secretary through which chemical facilities provide information to the Department for use pursuant to Sec. 27.200 of these regulations.

Under Secretary shall mean the Under Secretary for National Protection and Programs, Department of Homeland Security or any successors to that position within the Department or his designee.

Sec. 27.110 Applicability.

(a) This Part applies to chemical facilities and to covered facilities as set out herein.

(b) This Part does not apply to facilities regulated pursuant to the Maritime Transportation Security Act of 2002, Pub. L. 107-295, as amended; Public Water Systems, as defined by Section 1401 of the Safe Drinking Water Act, Pub. L. 93-523, as amended; Treatment Works as defined in Section 212 of the Federal Water Pollution Control Act, Pub. L. 92-500, as amended; any facility owned or operated by the Department of Defense or the Department of Energy, or any facility subject to regulation by the Nuclear Regulatory Commission.

Sec. 27.115 Implementation.

The Assistant Secretary may implement the Section 550 program in a phased manner, selecting certain chemical facilities for expedited initial processes under these regulations and identifying other chemical facilities or types or classes of chemical facilities for other phases of program implementation. The Assistant Secretary has flexibility to designate particular chemical facilities for specific phases of program implementation based on potential risk or any other factor consistent with this Part.

Sec. 27.120 Designation of a coordinating official; Consultations and technical assistance.

(a) The Assistant Secretary will designate a Coordinating Official who will be responsible for ensuring that these regulations are implemented in a uniform, impartial, and fair manner.

(b) The Coordinating Official and his staff shall provide guidance to covered facilities regarding compliance with this Part and shall, as necessary and to the extent that resources permit, be available to consult and to provide technical assistance to an owner or operator who seeks such consultation or assistance.

(c) In order to initiate consultations or seek technical assistance, a covered facility shall submit a written request for consultation or technical assistance to the Coordinating Official or contact the Department in any other manner specified in any subsequent guidance. Requests for consultation or technical guidance do not serve to toll any of the applicable timelines set forth in this Part.

(d) If a covered facility modifies its facility, processes, or the types or quantities of materials that it possesses, and believes that such changes may impact the covered facility's obligations under this Part, the covered facility may request a consultation with the Coordinating Official as specified in paragraph (c).

Sec. 27.125 Severability.

If a court finds any portion of this Part to have been promulgated without proper authority, the remainder of this Part will remain in full effect.

Subpart B--Chemical Facility Security Program

Sec. 27.200 Information regarding security risk for a chemical facility.

(a) Information to determine security risk. In order to determine the security risk posed by chemical facilities, the Secretary may, at any time, request information from chemical facilities that may reflect potential consequences of or vulnerabilities to a terrorist attack or incident, including questions specifically related to the nature of the business and activities conducted at the facility; information concerning the names, nature, conditions of storage, quantities, volumes, properties, customers, major uses, and other pertinent information about specific chemicals or chemicals meeting a specific criterion; information concerning facilities' security, safety, and emergency response practices, operations, and procedures; information regarding incidents, history, funding, and other matters bearing on the effectiveness of the security, safety and emergency response programs, and other information as necessary.

(b) Obtaining information from facilities.

(1) The Assistant Secretary may seek the information provided in paragraph (a) of this section by contacting chemical facilities individually or by publishing a notice in the Federal Register seeking information from chemical facilities that meet certain criteria, which the Department will use to determine risk profiles. Through any such individual or Federal Register notification, the Assistant Secretary may instruct such facilities to complete and submit a Top-Screen process, which may be completed through a secure Department Web site or through other

means approved by the Assistant Secretary.

(2) A facility must complete and submit a Top-Screen in accordance with the schedule provided in Sec. 27.210 if it possesses any of the chemicals listed in Appendix A to this part at the corresponding Screening Threshold Quantities.

(3) Where the Department requests that a facility complete and submit a Top-Screen, the facility must designate a person who is responsible for the submission of information through the CSAT system and who attests to the accuracy of the information contained in any CSAT submissions. Such submitter must be an officer of the corporation or other person designated by an officer of the corporation and must be domiciled in the United States.

(c) Presumptively High Risk Facilities.

(1) If a chemical facility subject to paragraph (a) or (b) of this section fails to provide information requested or complete the Top-Screen within the timeframe provided in Sec. 27.210, the Assistant Secretary may, after attempting to consult with the facility, reach a preliminary determination, based on the information then available, that the facility presumptively presents a high level of security risk. The Assistant Secretary shall then issue a notice to the entity of this determination and, if necessary, order the facility to provide information or complete the Top-Screen pursuant to these rules. If the facility then fails to do so, it may be subject to civil penalties pursuant to Sec. 27.300, audit and inspection under Sec. 27.250 or, if appropriate, an order to cease operations under Sec. 27.300.

(2) If the facility deemed ``presumptively high risk'' pursuant to paragraph (c)(1) of this section completes the Top-Screen, and the Department determines that it does not present a high level of security risk under Sec. 27.205, its status as ``presumptively high risk'' will terminate, and the Department will issue a notice to the facility to that effect.

Sec. 27.205 Determination that a chemical facility "presents a high level of security risk."

(a) Initial Determination. The Assistant Secretary may determine at any time that a chemical facility presents a high level of security risk based on any information available (including any information submitted to the Department under Sec. 27.200) that, in the Secretary's discretion, indicates the potential that a terrorist attack involving the facility could result in significant adverse consequences for human life or health, national security or critical economic assets. Upon determining that a facility presents a high level of security risk, the Department shall notify the facility in writing of such initial determination and may also notify the facility of the Department's preliminary determination of the facility's placement in a risk-based tier pursuant to Sec. 27.220(a).

(b) Redetermination. If a covered facility previously determined to present a high level of security risk has materially altered its operations, it may seek a redetermination by filing a Request for Redetermination with the Assistant Secretary, and may request a meeting regarding the Request. Within 45 calendar days of receipt of such a Request, or within 45 calendar days of a meeting under this paragraph, the Assistant Secretary shall notify the covered facility in writing of the Department's decision on the Request for Redetermination.

Sec. 27.210 Submissions schedule.

(a) Initial Submission. The timeframes in paragraphs (a)(2) and (a)(3) of this section also apply to covered facilities that submit an Alternative Security Program pursuant to Sec. 27.235.

    (1) Top-Screen. Facilities shall complete and submit a Top-Screen within the following time frames:

        (i) This paragraph is operative on the date that the Department publishes a final Appendix A. Unless otherwise notified, within 60 calendar days of the effective date of Appendix A for facilities that possess

any of the chemicals listed in Appendix A at the corresponding STQs, or within 60 calendar days for facilities that come into possession of any of the chemicals listed in Appendix A at the corresponding STQs; or

    (ii) Within the time frame provided in any written notification from the Department or specified in any subsequent Federal Register notice.

(2) Security Vulnerability Assessment. Unless otherwise notified, a covered facility must complete and submit a Security Vulnerability Assessment within 90 calendar days of written notification from the Department or within the time frame specified in any subsequent Federal Register notice.

(3) Site Security Plan. Unless otherwise notified, a covered facility must complete and submit a Site Security Plan within 120 calendar days of written notification from the Department or within the time frame specified in any subsequent Federal Register notice.

(b) Resubmission Schedule for Covered Facilities. The timeframes in this subsection also apply to covered facilities who submit an Alternative Security Program pursuant to Sec. 27.235.

(1) Top-Screen. Unless otherwise notified, Tier 1 and Tier 2 covered facilities must complete and submit a new Top-Screen no less than two years, and no more than two years and 60 calendar days, from the date of the Department's approval of the facility's Site Security Plan; and Tier 3 and Tier 4 covered facilities must complete and submit a Top-Screen no less than 3 years, and no more than 3 years and 60 calendar days, from the date of the Department's approval of the facility's Site Security Plan.

(2) Security Vulnerability Assessment. Unless otherwise notified and following a Top-Screen resubmission pursuant to paragraph (b)(1) of this section, a covered facility must complete and submit a new Security Vulnerability

Assessment within 90 calendar days of written notification from the Department or within the time frame specified in any subsequent Federal Register notice.

(3) Site Security Plan. Unless otherwise notified and following a Security Vulnerability Assessment resubmission pursuant to paragraph (b)(2) of this section , a covered facility must complete and submit a new Site Security Plan within 120 calendar days of written notification from the Department or within the time frame specified in any subsequent Federal Register notice.

(c) The Assistant Secretary retains the authority to modify the schedule in this Part as needed. The Assistant Secretary may shorten or extend these time periods based on the operations at the facility, the nature of the covered facility's vulnerabilities, the level and immediacy of security risk, or for other reasons. If the Department alters the time periods for a specific facility, the Department will do so in written notice to the facility.

(d) If a covered facility makes material modifications to its operations or site, the covered facility must complete and submit a revised Top-Screen to the Department within 60 days of the material modification. In accordance with the resubmission requirements in Sec. 27.210(b)(2) and (3), the Department will notify the covered facility as to whether the covered facility must submit a revised Security Vulnerability Assessment, Site Security Plan, or both.

Sec. 27.215 Security vulnerability assessments.

(a) Initial Assessment. If the Assistant Secretary determines that a chemical facility is high-risk, the facility must complete a Security Vulnerability Assessment. A Security Vulnerability Assessment shall include:

(1) Asset Characterization, which includes the identification and characterization of potential critical assets; identification of hazards and consequences of concern for the facility, its surroundings, its identified critical asset(s), and its supporting infrastructure; and identification of

existing layers of protection;

(2) Threat Assessment, which includes a description of possible internal threats, external threats, and internally-assisted threats;

(3) Security Vulnerability Analysis, which includes the identification of potential security vulnerabilities and the identification of existing countermeasures and their level of effectiveness in both reducing identified vulnerabilities and in meeting the applicable Risk-Based Performance Standards;

(4) Risk Assessment, including a determination of the relative degree of risk to the facility in terms of the expected effect on each critical asset and the likelihood of a success of an attack; and

(5) Countermeasures Analysis, including strategies that reduce the probability of a successful attack or reduce the probable degree of success, strategies that enhance the degree of risk reduction, the reliability and maintainability of the options, the capabilities and effectiveness of mitigation options, and the feasibility of the options.

(b) Except as provided in Sec. 27.235, a covered facility must complete the Security Vulnerability Assessment through the CSAT process, or through any other methodology or process identified or issued by the Assistant Secretary.

(c) Covered facilities must submit a Security Vulnerability Assessment to the Department in accordance with the schedule provided in Sec. 27.210.

(d) Updates and Revisions.

(1) A covered facility must update and revise its Security Vulnerability Assessment in accordance with the schedule provided in Sec. 27.210.

(2) Notwithstanding paragraph (d)(1) of this section, a covered facility must update, revise or otherwise alter its Security Vulnerability Assessment to account for new or differing modes of potential terrorist attack or for other security-related reasons, if requested by the Assistant Secretary.

Sec. 27.220 Tiering.

(a) Preliminary Determination of Risk-Based Tiering. Based on the information the Department receives in accordance with Sec. Sec. 27.200 and 27.205 (including information submitted through the Top-Screen process) and following its initial determination in Sec. 27.205(a) that a facility presents a high level of security risk, the Department shall notify a facility of the Department's preliminary determination of the facility's placement in a risk-based tier.

(b) Confirmation or Alteration of Risk-Based Tiering. Following review of a covered facility's Security Vulnerability Assessment, the Assistant Secretary shall notify the covered facility of its final placement within a risk-based tier, or for covered facilities previously notified of a preliminary tiering, confirm or alter such tiering.

(c) The Department shall place covered facilities in one of four risk-based tiers, ranging from highest risk facilities in Tier 1 to lowest risk facilities in Tier 4.

(d) The Assistant Secretary may provide the facility with guidance regarding the risk-based performance standards and any other necessary guidance materials applicable to its assigned tier.

Sec. 27.225 Site security plans.

(a) The Site Security Plan must meet the following standards:
  (1) Address each vulnerability identified in the facility's Security Vulnerability Assessment, and identify and describe the security measures to address each such vulnerability;
  (2) Identify and describe how security measures selected by the facility will address the applicable risk-based performance standards and potential modes of terrorist attack including, as applicable, vehicle-borne explosive devices, water-borne explosive devices, ground assault, or other modes or

potential modes identified by the Department;

    (3) Identify and describe how security measures selected and utilized by the facility will meet or exceed each applicable performance standard for the appropriate risk-based tier for the facility; and

    (4) Specify other information the Assistant Secretary deems necessary regarding chemical facility security.

  (b) Except as provided in Sec. 27.235, a covered facility must complete the Site Security Plan through the CSAT process, or through any other methodology or process identified or issued by the Assistant Secretary.

  (c) Covered facilities must submit a Site Security Plan to the Department in accordance with the schedule provided in Sec. 27.210.

  (d) Updates and Revisions.

    (1) When a covered facility updates, revises or otherwise alters its Security Vulnerability Assessment pursuant to Sec. 27.215(d), the covered facility shall make corresponding changes to its Site Security Plan.

    (2) A covered facility must also update and revise its Site Security Plan in accordance with the schedule in Sec. 27.210.

  (e) A covered facility must conduct an annual audit of its compliance with its Site Security Plan.

Sec. 27.230 Risk-based performance standards.

  (a) Covered facilities must satisfy the performance standards identified in this section. The Assistant Secretary will issue guidance on the application of these standards to risk-based tiers of covered facilities, and the acceptable layering of measures used to meet these standards will vary by risk-based tier. Each covered facility must select, develop in their Site Security Plan, and implement appropriately risk-based measures designed to satisfy the following performance standards:

    (1) Restrict Area Perimeter. Secure and monitor the perimeter

of the facility;

(2) Secure Site Assets. Secure and monitor restricted areas or potentially critical targets within the facility;

(3) Screen and Control Access. Control access to the facility and to restricted areas within the facility by screening and/or inspecting individuals and vehicles as they enter, including,

    (i) Measures to deter the unauthorized introduction of dangerous substances and devices that may facilitate an attack or actions having serious negative consequences for the population surrounding the facility; and

    (ii) Measures implementing a regularly updated identification system that checks the identification of facility personnel and other persons seeking access to the facility and that discourages abuse through established disciplinary measures;

(4) Deter, Detect, and Delay. Deter, detect, and delay an attack, creating sufficient time between detection of an attack and the point at which the attack becomes successful, including measures to:

    (i) Deter vehicles from penetrating the facility perimeter, gaining unauthorized access to restricted areas or otherwise presenting a hazard to potentially critical targets;

    (ii) Deter attacks through visible, professional, well maintained security measures and systems, including security personnel, detection systems, barriers and barricades, and hardened or reduced value targets;

    (iii) Detect attacks at early stages, through countersurveillance, frustration of opportunity to observe potential targets, surveillance and sensing systems, and barriers and barricades; and

    (iv) Delay an attack for a sufficient period of time so to allow appropriate response through on-site security response, barriers and barricades, hardened targets, and well-coordinated response planning;

(5) Shipping, Receipt, and Storage. Secure and monitor the

shipping, receipt, and storage of hazardous materials for the facility;

(6) Theft and Diversion. Deter theft or diversion of potentially dangerous chemicals;

(7) Sabotage. Deter insider sabotage;

(8) Cyber. Deter cyber sabotage, including by preventing unauthorized onsite or remote access to critical process controls, such as Supervisory Control and Data Acquisition (SCADA) systems, Distributed Control Systems (DCS), Process Control Systems (PCS), Industrial Control Systems (ICS), critical business system, and other sensitive computerized systems;

(9) Response. Develop and exercise an emergency plan to respond to security incidents internally and with assistance of local law enforcement and first responders;

(10) Monitoring. Maintain effective monitoring, communications and warning systems, including,

    (i) Measures designed to ensure that security systems and equipment are in good working order and inspected, tested, calibrated, and otherwise maintained;

    (ii) Measures designed to regularly test security systems, note deficiencies, correct for detected deficiencies, and record results so that they are available for inspection by the Department; and

    (iii) Measures to allow the facility to promptly identify and respond to security system and equipment failures or malfunctions;

(11) Training. Ensure proper security training, exercises, and drills of facility personnel;

(12) Personnel Surety. Perform appropriate background checks on and ensure appropriate credentials for facility personnel, and as appropriate, for unescorted visitors with access to restricted areas or critical assets, including,

    (i) Measures designed to verify and validate identity;

    (ii) Measures designed to check criminal history;

    (iii) Measures designed to verify and validate legal

authorization to work; and
(iv) Measures designed to identify people with terrorist ties;
(13) Elevated Threats. Escalate the level of protective measures for periods of elevated threat;
(14) Specific Threats, Vulnerabilities, or Risks. Address specific threats, vulnerabilities or risks identified by the Assistant Secretary for the particular facility at issue;
(15) Reporting of Significant Security Incidents. Report significant security incidents to the Department and to local law enforcement officials;
(16) Significant Security Incidents and Suspicious Activities. Identify, investigate, report, and maintain records of significant security incidents and suspicious activities in or near the site;
(17) Officials and Organization. Establish official(s) and an organization responsible for security and for compliance with these standards;
(18) Records. Maintain appropriate records; and
(19) Address any additional performance standards the Assistant Secretary may specify.
(b) [Reserved]

Sec. 27.235 Alternative security program.

(a) Covered facilities may submit an Alternate Security Program (ASP) pursuant to the requirements of this section. The Assistant Secretary may approve an Alternate Security Program, in whole, in part, or subject to revisions or supplements, upon a determination that the Alternate Security Program meets the requirements of this Part and provides for an equivalent level of security to that established by this Part.

(1) A Tier 4 facility may submit an ASP in lieu of a Security Vulnerability Assessment, Site Security Plan, or both.
(2) Tier 1, Tier 2, or Tier 3 facilities may submit an ASP in lieu of a Site Security Plan. Tier 1, Tier 2, and Tier 3 facilities may not submit an ASP in lieu of a Security Vulnerability

Assessment.

(b) The Department will provide notice to a covered facility about the approval or disapproval, in whole or in part, of an ASP, using the procedure specified in Sec. 27.240 if the ASP is intended to take the place of a Security Vulnerability Assessment or using the procedure specified in Sec. 27.245 if the ASP is intended to take the place of a Site Security Plan.

Sec. 27.240 Review and approval of security vulnerability assessments.

(a) Review and Approval. The Department will review and approve in writing all Security Vulnerability Assessments that satisfy the requirements of Sec. 27.215, including Alternative Security Programs submitted pursuant to Sec. 27.235.

(b) If a Security Vulnerability Assessment does not satisfy the requirements of Sec. 27.215, the Department will provide the facility with a written notification that includes a clear explanation of deficiencies in the Security Vulnerability Assessment. The facility shall then enter further consultations with the Department and resubmit a sufficient Security Vulnerability Assessment by the time specified in the written notification provided by the Department under this section. If the resubmitted Security Vulnerability Assessment does not satisfy the requirements of Sec. 27.215, the Department will provide the facility with written notification (including a clear explanation of deficiencies in the SVA) of the Department's disapproval of the SVA.

Sec. 27.245 Review and approval of site security plans.

(a) Review and Approval.
  (1) The Department will review and approve or disapprove all Site Security Plans that satisfy the requirements of Sec. 27.225, including Alternative Security Programs submitted pursuant to Sec. 27.235.
     (i) The Department will review Site Security Plans through

a two-step process. Upon receipt of Site Security Plan from the covered facility, the Department will review the documentation and make a preliminary determination as to whether it satisfies the requirements of Sec. 27.225. If the Department finds that the requirements are satisfied, the Department will issue a Letter of Authorization to the covered facility.

(ii) Following issuance of the Letter of Authorization, the Department will inspect the covered facility in accordance with Sec. 27.250 for purposes of determining compliance with the requirements of this Part.

(iii) If the Department approves the Site Security Plan in accordance with Sec. 27.250, the Department will issue a Letter of Approval to the facility, and the facility shall implement the approved Site Security Plan.

(2) The Department will not disapprove a Site Security Plan submitted under this Part based on the presence or absence of a particular security measure. The Department may disapprove a Site Security Plan that fails to satisfy the risk-based performance standards established in Sec. 27.230.

(b) When the Department disapproves a preliminary Site Security Plan issued prior to inspection or a Site Security Plan following inspection, the Department will provide the facility with a written notification that includes a clear explanation of deficiencies in the Site Security Plan. The facility shall then enter further consultations with the Department and resubmit a sufficient Site Security Plan by the time specified in the written notification provided by the Department under this section. If the resubmitted Site Security Plan does not satisfy the requirements of Sec. 27.225, the Department will provide the facility with written notification (including a clear explanation of deficiencies in the SSP) of the Department's disapproval of the SSP.

Sec. 27.250 Inspections and audits.

(a) Authority. In order to assess compliance with the requirements of this Part, authorized Department officials may enter, inspect, and audit the property, equipment, operations, and records of covered facilities.

(b) Following preliminary approval of a Site Security Plan in accordance with Sec. 27.245, the Department will inspect the covered facility for purposes of determining compliance with the requirements of this Part.

  (1) If after the inspection, the Department determines that the requirements of Sec. 27.225 have been met, the Department will issue a Letter of Approval to the covered facility.

  (2) If after the inspection, the Department determines that the requirements of Sec. 27.225 have not been met, the Department will proceed as directed by Sec. 27.245(b) in ``Review and Approval of Site Security Plans."

(c) Time and Manner. Authorized Department officials will conduct audits and inspections at reasonable times and in a reasonable manner. The Department will provide covered facility owners and/or operators with 24-hour advance notice before inspections, except

  (1) If the Under Secretary or Assistant Secretary determines that an inspection without such notice is warranted by exigent circumstances and approves such inspection; or

  (2) If any delay in conducting an inspection might be seriously detrimental to security, and the Director of the Chemical Security Division determines that an inspection without notice is warranted, and approves an inspector to conduct such inspection.

(d) Inspectors. Inspections and audits are conducted by personnel duly authorized and designated for that purpose as ``inspectors" by the Secretary or the Secretary's designee.

  (1) An inspector will, on request, present his or her credentials for examination, but the credentials may not be reproduced by the facility.

(2) An inspector may administer oaths and receive affirmations, with the consent of any witness, in any matter.

(3) An inspector may gather information by reasonable means including, but not limited to, interviews, statements, photocopying, photography, and video- and audio-recording. All documents, objects and electronically stored information collected by each inspector during the performance of that inspector's duties shall be maintained for a reasonable period of time in the files of the Department of Homeland Security maintained for that facility or matter.

(4) An inspector may request forthwith access to all records required to be kept pursuant to Sec. 27.255. An inspector shall be provided with the immediate use of any photocopier or other equipment necessary to copy any such record. If copies can not be provided immediately upon request, the inspector shall be permitted immediately to take the original records for duplication and prompt return.

(e) Confidentiality. In addition to the protections provided under CVI in Sec. 27.400, information received in an audit or inspection under this section, including the identity of the persons involved in the inspection or who provide information during the inspection, shall remain confidential under the investigatory file exception, or other appropriate exception, to the public disclosure requirements of 5 U.S.C. 552.

(f) Guidance. The Assistant Secretary shall issue guidance identifying appropriate processes for such inspections, and specifying the type and nature of documentation that must be made available for review during inspections and audits.

Sec. 27.255 Recordkeeping requirements.

(a) Except as provided in Sec. 27.255(b), the covered facility must keep records of the activities as set out below for at least three years and make them available to the Department upon request. A covered facility must keep the following records:

(1) Training. For training, the date and location of each session, time of day and duration of session, a description of the training, the name and qualifications of the instructor, a clear, legible list of attendees to include the attendee signature, at least one other unique identifier of each attendee receiving the training, and the results of any evaluation or testing.

(2) Drills and exercises. For each drill or exercise, the date held, a description of the drill or exercise, a list of participants, a list of equipment (other than personal equipment) tested or employed in the exercise, the name(s) and qualifications of the exercise director, and any best practices or lessons learned which may improve the Site Security Plan;

(3) Incidents and breaches of security. Date and time of occurrence, location within the facility, a description of the incident or breach, the identity of the individual to whom it was reported, and a description of the response;

(4) Maintenance, calibration, and testing of security equipment. The date and time, name and qualifications of the technician(s) doing the work, and the specific security equipment involved for each occurrence of maintenance, calibration, and testing;

(5) Security threats. Date and time of occurrence, how the threat was communicated, who received or identified the threat, a description of the threat, to whom it was reported, and a description of the response;

(6) Audits. For each audit of a covered facility's Site Security Plan (including each audit required under Sec. 27.225(e)) or Security Vulnerability Assessment, a record of the audit, including the date of the audit, results of the audit, name(s) of the person(s) who conducted the audit, and a letter certified by the covered facility stating the date the audit was conducted.

(7) Letters of Authorization and Approval. All Letters of Authorization and Approval from the Department, and documentation identifying the results of audits and

inspections conducted pursuant to Sec. 27.250.

(b) A covered facility must retain records of submitted Top-Screens, Security Vulnerability Assessments, Site Security Plans, and all related correspondence with the Department for at least six years and make them available to the Department upon request.

(c) To the extent necessary for security purposes, the Department may request that a covered facility make available records kept pursuant to other Federal programs or regulations.

(d) Records required by this section may be kept in electronic format. If kept in an electronic format, they must be protected against unauthorized access, deletion, destruction, amendment, and disclosure.

Subpart C--Orders and Adjudications

Sec. 27.300 Orders.

(a) Orders Generally. When the Assistant Secretary determines that a facility is in violation of any of the requirements of this Part, the Assistant Secretary may take appropriate action including the issuance of an appropriate Order.

(b) Orders Assessing Civil Penalty and Orders to Cease Operations.

    (1) Where the Assistant Secretary determines that a facility is in violation of an Order issued pursuant to paragraph (a) of this section, the Assistant may enter an Order Assessing Civil Penalty, Order to Cease Operations, or both.

    (2) Following the issuance of an Order by the Assistant Secretary pursuant to paragraph (b)(1) of this section, the facility may enter further consultations with Department.

    (3) Where the Assistant Secretary determines that a facility is in violation of an Order issued pursuant to paragraph (a) of this section and issues an Order Assessing Civil Penalty pursuant to paragraph (b)(1) of this section, a chemical facility is liable to the United States for a civil penalty of not more than $25,000 for each day during which the violation

continues.

(c) Procedures for Orders.

   (1) At a minimum, an Order shall be signed by the Assistant Secretary, shall be dated, and shall include:

      (i) The name and address of the facility in question;

      (ii) A listing of the provision(s) that the facility is alleged to have violated;

      (iii) A statement of facts upon which the alleged instances of noncompliance are based;

      (iv) A clear explanation of deficiencies in the facility's chemical security program, including, if applicable, any deficiencies in the facility's Security Vulnerability Assessment, Site Security Plan, or both; and

      (v) A statement, indicating what action(s) the chemical must take to remedy the instance(s) of noncompliance; and

      (vi) The date by which the facility must comply with the terms of the Order.

   (2) The Assistant Secretary may establish procedures for the issuance of Orders.

(d) A facility must comply with the terms of the Order by the date specified in the Order unless the facility has filed a timely Notice for Application for Review under Sec. 27.310.

(e) Where a facility or other person contests the determination of the Assistant Secretary to issue an Order, a chemical facility may seek an adjudication pursuant to Sec. 27.310.

(f) An Order issued under this section becomes final agency action when the time to file a Notice of Application of Review under Sec. 27.310 has passed without such a filing or upon the conclusion of adjudication or appeal proceedings under this subpart.

Sec. 27.305 Neutral adjudications.

(a) Any facility or other person who has received a Finding pursuant to Sec. 27.230(a)(12)(iv), a Determination pursuant to Sec. 27.245(b), or an Order pursuant to Sec. 27.300 is entitled to an

adjudication, by a neutral adjudications officer, of any issue of material fact relevant to any administrative action which deprives that person of a cognizable interest in liberty or property.

(b) A neutral adjudications officer appointed pursuant to Sec. 27.315 shall issue an Initial Decision on any material factual issue related to a Finding pursuant to Sec. 27.230(a)(12)(iv), a Determination pursuant to Sec. 27.245, or an Order pursuant to Sec. 27.300 before any such administrative action is reviewed on appeal pursuant to Sec. 27.345.

Sec. 27.310 Commencement of adjudication proceedings.

(a) Proceedings Instituted by Facilities or other Persons. A facility or other person may institute proceedings to review a determination by the Assistant Secretary:
  (1) Finding, pursuant to the Sec. 27.230(a)(12)(iv), that an individual is a potential security threat;
  (2) Disapproving a Site Security Plan pursuant to Sec. 27.245(b); or
  (3) Issuing an Order pursuant to Sec. 27.300(a) or (b).
(b) Procedure for Applications by Facilities or other Persons. A facility or other person may institute Proceedings by filing a Notice of Application for Review specifying that the facility or other person requests a Proceeding to review a determination specified in paragraph (a) of this section.
  (1) An Applicant institutes a Proceeding by filing a Notice of Application for Review with the office of the Department hereinafter designated by the Secretary.
  (2) An Applicant must file a Notice of Application for Review within seven calendar days of notification to the facility or other person of the Assistant Secretary's Finding, Determination, or Order.
  (3) The Applicant shall file and simultaneously serve each Notice of Application for Review and all subsequent filings on the Assistant Secretary and the General Counsel.
  (4) An Order is stayed from the timely filing of a Notice of

Application for Review until the Presiding Officer issues an Initial Decision, unless the Secretary has lifted the stay due to exigent circumstances pursuant to paragraph (d) of this section.

(5) The Applicant shall file and serve an Application for Review within fourteen calendar days of the notification to the facility or other person of the Assistant Secretary's Finding, Determination, or Order.

(6) Each Application for Review shall be accompanied by all legal memoranda, other documents, declarations, affidavits, and other evidence supporting the position asserted by the Applicant.

(c) Response. The Assistant Secretary, through the Office of General Counsel, shall file and serve a Response, accompanied by all legal memoranda, other documents, declarations, affidavits and other evidence supporting the position asserted by the Assistant Secretary within fourteen calendar days of the filing and service of the Application for Review and all supporting papers.

(d) Procedural Modifications. The Secretary may, in exigent circumstances (as determined in his sole discretion):

(1) Lift any stay applicable to any Order under Sec. 27.300;

(2) Modify the time for a response;

(3) Rule on the sufficiency of Applications for Review; or

(4) Otherwise modify these procedures with respect to particular matters.

Sec. 27.315 Presiding officers for proceedings.

(a) Immediately upon the filing of any Application for Review, the Secretary shall appoint an attorney, who is employed by the Department and who has not performed any investigative or prosecutorial function with respect to the matter, to act as a neutral adjudications officer or Presiding Officer for the compilation of a factual record and the recommendation of an Initial Decision for each Proceeding.

(b) Notwithstanding paragraph (a) of this section, the Secretary

may appoint one or more attorneys who are employed by the Department and who do not perform any investigative or prosecutorial function with respect to this subpart, to serve generally in the capacity as Presiding Officer(s) for such matters pursuant to such procedures as the Secretary may hereafter establish.

Sec. 27.320 Prohibition on ex parte communications during proceedings.

(a) At no time after the designation of a Presiding Officer for a Proceeding and prior to the issuance of a Final Decision pursuant to Sec. 27.345 with respect to a facility or other person, shall the appointed Presiding Officer, or any person who will advise that official in the decision on the matter, discuss ex parte the merits of the proceeding with any interested person outside the Department, with any Department official who performs a prosecutorial or investigative function in such proceeding or a factually related proceeding, or with any representative of such person.

(b) If, after appointment of a Presiding Officer and prior to the issuance of a Final Decision pursuant to Sec. 27.345 with respect to a facility or other person, the appointed Presiding Officer, or any person who will advise that official in the decision on the matter, receives from or on behalf of any party, by means of an ex parte communication, information which is relevant to the decision of the matter and to which other parties have not had an opportunity to respond, a summary of such information shall be served on all other parties, who shall have an opportunity to reply to the ex parte communication within a time set by the Presiding Officer.

(c) The consideration of classified information or CVI pursuant to an in camera procedure does not constitute a prohibited ex parte communication for purposes of this subpart.

Sec. 27.325 Burden of proof.

The Assistant Secretary bears the initial burden of proving the facts necessary to support the challenged administrative action at

every proceeding instituted under this subpart.

Sec. 27.330 Summary decision procedures.

(a) The Presiding Officer appointed for each Proceeding shall immediately consider whether the summary adjudication of the Application for Review is appropriate based on the Application for Review, the Response, and all the supporting filings of the parties pursuant to Sec. Sec. 27.310(b)(5) and 27.310(c).

    (1) The Presiding Officer shall promptly issue any necessary scheduling order for any additional briefing of the issue of summary adjudication on the Application for Review and Response.

    (2) The Presiding Officer may conduct scheduling conferences and other proceedings that the Presiding Officer determines to be appropriate.

(b) If the Presiding Officer determines that there is no genuine issue of material fact and that one party or the other is entitled to decision as a matter of law, then the record shall be closed and the Presiding Officer shall issue an Initial Decision on the Application for Review pursuant to Sec. 27.340.

(c) If a Presiding Officer determines that any factual issues require the cross-examination of one or more witnesses or other proceedings at a hearing, the Presiding Officer, in consultation with the parties, shall promptly schedule a hearing to be conducted pursuant to Sec. 27.335.

Sec. 27.335 Hearing procedures.

(a) Any hearing shall be held as expeditiously as possible at the location most conducive to a prompt presentation of any necessary testimony or other proceedings.

    (1) Videoconferencing and teleconferencing may be used where appropriate at the discretion of the Presiding Officer.

    (2) Each party offering the affirmative testimony of a witness shall present that testimony by declaration, affidavit, or

other sworn statement submitted in advance as ordered by
the Presiding Officer.

(3) Any witness presented for further examination shall be
asked to testify under an oath or affirmation.

(4) The hearing shall be recorded verbatim.

(b)

(1) A facility or other person may appear and be heard on his
own behalf or through any counsel of his choice who is
qualified to possess CVI.

(2) A facility of other person individually, or through counsel,
may offer relevant and material information including
written direct testimony which he believes should be
considered in opposition to the administrative action or
which may bear on the sanction being sought.

(3) The facility or other person individually, or through counsel,
may conduct such cross-examination as may be specifically
allowed by the Presiding Officer for a full determination of
the facts.

Sec. 27.340 Completion of adjudication proceedings.

(a) The Presiding Officer shall close and certify the record of the
adjudication promptly upon the completion of:

(1) Summary judgment proceedings,

(2) A hearing, if necessary,

(3) The submission of post hearing briefs, if any are ordered by
the Presiding Officer, and

(4) The conclusion of oral arguments, if any are permitted by
the Presiding Officer.

(b) The Presiding Officer shall issue an Initial Decision based on
the certified record, and the decision shall be subject to appeal
pursuant to Sec. 27.345.

(c) An Initial Decision shall become a final agency action on the
expiration of the time for an Appeal pursuant to Sec. 27.345.

Sec. 27.345 Appeals.

(a) Right to Appeal. A facility or any person who has received an Initial Decision under Sec. 27.340(b) has the right to appeal to the Under Secretary acting as a neutral appeals officer.

(b) Procedure for Appeals.

(1) The Assistant Secretary, a facility or other person, or a representative on behalf of a facility or person, may institute an Appeal by filing a Notice of Appeal with the office of the Department hereinafter designated by the Secretary.

(2) The Assistant Secretary, a facility, or other person must file a Notice of Appeal within seven calendar days of the service of the Presiding Officer's Initial Decision.

(3) The Appellant shall file with the designated office and simultaneously serve each Notice of Appeal and all subsequent filings on the General Counsel.

(4) An Initial Decision is stayed from the timely filing of a Notice of Appeal until the Under Secretary issues a Final Decision, unless the Secretary lifts the stay due to exigent circumstances pursuant to Sec. 27.310(d).

(5) The Appellant shall file and serve a Brief within 28 calendar days of the notification of the service of the Presiding Officer's Initial Decision.

(6) The Appellee shall file and serve its Opposition Brief within 28 calendar days of the service of the Appellant's Brief.

(c) The Under Secretary may provide for an expedited appeal for appropriate matters.

(d) Ex Parte Communications.

(1) At no time after the filing of a Notice of Appeal pursuant to paragraph (b)(1) of this section and prior to the issuance of a Final Decision on an Appeal pursuant to paragraph (f) of this section with respect to a facility or other person shall the Under Secretary, his designee, or any person who will advise that official in the decision on the matter, discuss ex parte the merits of the proceeding with any interested person outside the Department, with any Department official who

performs a prosecutorial or investigative function in such proceeding or a factually related proceeding, or with any representative of such person.

(2) If, after the filing of a Notice of Appeal pursuant to paragraph (b)(1) of this section and prior to the issuance of a Final Decision on an Appeal pursuant to paragraph (f) of this section with respect to a facility or other person, the Under Secretary, his designee, or any person who will advise that official in the decision on the matter, receives from or on behalf of any party, by means of an ex parte communication, information which is relevant to the decision of the matter and to which other parties have not had an opportunity to respond, a summary of such information shall be served on all other parties, who shall have an opportunity to reply to the ex parte communication within a time set by the Under Secretary or his designee.

(3) The consideration of classified information or CVI pursuant to an in camera procedure does not constitute a prohibited ex parte communication for purposes of this subpart.

(e) A facility or other person may elect to have the Under Secretary participate in any mediation or other resolution process by expressly waiving, in writing, any argument that such participation has compromised the Appeal process.

(f) The Under Secretary shall issue a Final Decision and serve it upon the parties. A Final Decision made by the Under Secretary constitutes final agency action.

(g) The Secretary may establish procedures for the conduct of Appeals pursuant to this section.

Subpart D--Other

Sec. 27.400 Chemical-terrorism vulnerability information.

(a) Applicability. This section governs the maintenance, safeguarding, and disclosure of information and records that constitute Chemical-terrorism Vulnerability Information (CVI), as

defined in Sec. 27.400(b). The Secretary shall administer this section consistent with Section 550(c) of the Homeland Security Appropriations Act of 2007, including appropriate sharing with Federal, State and local officials.

(b) Chemical-terrorism Vulnerability Information. In accordance with Section 550(c) of the Department of Homeland Security Appropriations Act of 2007, the following information, whether transmitted verbally, electronically, or in written form, shall constitute CVI:

(1) Security Vulnerability Assessments under Sec. 27.215;

(2) Site Security Plans under Sec. 27.225;

(3) Documents relating to the Department's review and approval of Security Vulnerability Assessments and Site Security Plans, including Letters of Authorization, Letters of Approval and responses thereto; written notices; and other documents developed pursuant to Sec. 27.240 or Sec. 27.245;

(4) Alternate Security Programs under Sec. 27.235;

(5) Documents relating to inspection or audits under Sec. 27.250;

(6) Any records required to be created or retained under Sec. 27.255;

(7) Sensitive portions of orders, notices or letters under Sec. 27.300;

(8) Information developed pursuant to Sec. Sec. 27.200 and 27.205; and

(9) Other information developed for chemical facility security purposes that the Secretary, in his discretion, determines is similar to the information protected in Sec. 27.400(b)(1) through (8) and thus warrants protection as CVI.

(c) Covered Persons. Persons subject to the requirements of this section are:

(1) Each person who has a need to know CVI, as specified in Sec. 27.400(e);

(2) Each person who otherwise receives or gains access to what they know or should reasonably know constitutes CVI.

(d) Duty to protect information. A covered person must--

(1) Take reasonable steps to safeguard CVI in that person's possession or control, including electronic data, from unauthorized disclosure. When a person is not in physical possession of CVI, the person must store it in a secure container, such as a safe, that limits access only to covered persons with a need to know;

(2) Disclose, or otherwise provide access to, CVI only to persons who have a need to know;

(3) Refer requests for CVI by persons without a need to know to the Assistant Secretary;

(4) Mark CVI as specified in Sec. 27.400(f);

(5) Dispose of CVI as specified in Sec. 27.400(k);

(6) If a covered person receives a record or verbal transmission containing CVI that is not marked as specified in Sec. 27.400(f), the covered person must--

(i) Mark the record as specified in Sec. 27.400(f) of this section; and

(ii) Inform the sender of the record that the record must be marked as specified in Sec. 27.400(f); or

(iii) If received verbally, make reasonable efforts to memorialize such information and mark the memorialized record as specified in Sec. 27.400(f) of this section, and inform the speaker of any determination that such information warrants CVI protection.

(7) When a covered person becomes aware that CVI has been released to persons without a need to know (including a covered person under Sec. 27.400(c)(2)), the covered person must promptly inform the Assistant Secretary.

(8) In the case of information that is CVI and also has been designated as critical infrastructure information under Section 214 of the Homeland Security Act, any covered person in possession of such information must comply with the disclosure restrictions and other requirements applicable to such information under Section 214 and any

implementing regulations.
(e) Need to know.
  (1) A person, including a State or local official, has a need to know CVI in each of the following circumstances:
    (i) When the person requires access to specific CVI to carry out chemical facility security activities approved, accepted, funded, recommended, or directed by the Department.
    (ii) When the person needs the information to receive training to carry out chemical facility security activities approved, accepted, funded, recommended, or directed by the Department.
    (iii) When the information is necessary for the person to supervise or otherwise manage individuals carrying out chemical facility security activities approved, accepted, funded, recommended, or directed by the Department.
    (iv) When the person needs the information to provide technical or legal advice to a covered person, who has a need to know the information, regarding chemical facility security requirements of Federal law.
    (v) When the Department determines that access is required under Sec. Sec. 27.400(h) or 27.400(i) in the course of a judicial or administrative proceeding.
  (2) Federal employees, contractors, and grantees.
    (i) A Federal employee has a need to know CVI if access to the information is necessary for performance of the employee's official duties.
    (ii) A person acting in the performance of a contract with or grant from the Department has a need to know CVI if access to the information is necessary to performance of the contract or grant. Contractors or grantees may not further disclose CVI without the consent of the Assistant Secretary.
    (iii) The Department may require that non-Federal persons seeking access to CVI complete a non-disclosure agreement before such access is granted.

(3) Background check. The Department may make an individual's access to the CVI contingent upon satisfactory completion of a security background check or other procedures and requirements for safeguarding CVI that are satisfactory to the Department.

(4) Need to know further limited by the Department. For some specific CVI, the Department may make a finding that only specific persons or classes of persons have a need to know.

(5) Nothing in Sec. 27.400(e) shall prevent the Department from determining, in its discretion, that a person not otherwise listed in Sec. 27.400(e) has a need to know CVI in a particular circumstance.

(f) Marking of paper records.

(1) In the case of paper records containing CVI, a covered person must mark the record by placing the protective marking conspicuously on the top, and the distribution limitation statement on the bottom, of--

    (i) The outside of any front and back cover, including a binder cover or folder, if the document has a front and back cover;

    (ii) Any title page; and

    (iii) Each page of the document.

(2) Protective marking. The protective marking is: CHEMICAL-TERRORISM VULNERABILITY INFORMATION.

(3) Distribution limitation statement. The distribution limitation statement is: WARNING: This record contains Chemical-terrorism Vulnerability Information controlled by 6 CFR 27.400. Do not disclose to persons without a ``need to know'' in accordance with 6 CFR 27.400(e). Unauthorized release may result in civil penalties or other action. In any administrative or judicial proceeding, this information shall be treated as classified information in accordance with 6 CFR 27.400(h) and (i).

(4) Other types of records. In the case of non-paper records that contain CVI, including motion picture films, videotape

recordings, audio recording, and electronic and magnetic records, a covered person must clearly and conspicuously mark the records with the protective marking and the distribution limitation statement such that the viewer or listener is reasonably likely to see or hear them when obtaining access to the contents of the record.

(g) Disclosure by the Department--In general.

(1) Except as otherwise provided in this section, and notwithstanding the Freedom of Information Act (5 U.S.C. 552), the Privacy Act (5 U.S.C. 552a), and other laws, records containing CVI are not available for public inspection or copying, nor does the Department release such records to persons without a need to know.

(2) Disclosure of Segregatable Information under the Freedom of Information Act and the Privacy Act. If a record is marked to signify both CVI and information that is not CVI, the Department, on a proper Freedom of Information Act or Privacy Act request, may disclose the record with the CVI redacted, provided the record is not otherwise exempt from disclosure under the Freedom of Information Act or Privacy Act.

(h) Disclosure in administrative enforcement proceedings.

(1) The Department may provide CVI to a person governed by Section 550, and his counsel, in the context of an administrative enforcement proceeding of Section 550 when, in the sole discretion of the Department, as appropriate, access to the CVI is necessary for the person to prepare a response to allegations contained in a legal enforcement action document issued by the Department.

(2) Security background check. Prior to providing CVI to a person under Sec. 27.400(h)(1), the Department may require the individual or, in the case of an entity, the individuals representing the entity, and their counsel, to undergo and satisfy, in the judgment of the Department, a security background check.

(i) Disclosure in judicial proceedings.

(1) In any judicial enforcement proceeding of Section 550, the Secretary, in his sole discretion, may, subject to Sec. 27.400(i)(1)(i), authorize access to CVI for persons necessary for the conduct of such proceedings, including such persons' counsel, provided that no other persons not so authorized shall have access to or be present for the disclosure of such information.

   (i) Security background check. Prior to providing CVI to a person under Sec. 27.400(i)(1), the Department may require the individual to undergo and satisfy, in the judgment of the Department, a security background check.

   (ii) [Reserved]

(2) In any judicial enforcement proceeding of Section 550 where a person seeks to disclose CVI to a person not authorized to receive it under paragraph (i)(1) of this section, or where a person not authorized to receive CVI under paragraph (i)(1) of this section seeks to compel its disclosure through discovery, the United States may make an ex parte application in writing to the court seeking authorization to--

   (i) Redact specified items of CVI from documents to be introduced into evidence or made available to the defendant through discovery under the Federal Rules of Civil Procedure;

   (ii) Substitute a summary of the information for such CVI; or

   (iii) Substitute a statement admitting relevant facts that the CVI would tend to prove.

(3) The court shall grant a request under paragraph (i)(2) of this section if, after in camera review, the court finds that the redacted item, stipulation, or summary is sufficient to allow the defendant to prepare a defense.

(4) If the court enters an order granting a request under paragraph (i)(2) of this section, the entire text of the documents to which the request relates shall be sealed and

preserved in the records of the court to be made available to the appellate court in the event of an appeal.

(5) If the court enters an order denying a request of the United States under paragraph (i)(2) of this section, the United States may take an immediate, interlocutory appeal of the court's order in accordance with 18 U.S.C. 2339B(f)(4), (5). For purposes of such an appeal, the entire text of the documents to which the request relates, together with any transcripts of arguments made ex parte to the court in connection therewith, shall be maintained under seal and delivered to the appellate court.

(6) Except as provided otherwise at the sole discretion of the Secretary, access to CVI shall not be available in any civil or criminal litigation unrelated to the enforcement of Section 550.

(7) Taking of trial testimony--
    (i) Objection--During the examination of a witness in any judicial proceeding, the United States may object to any question or line of inquiry that may require the witness to disclose CVI not previously found to be admissible.
    (ii) Action by court--In determining whether a response is admissible, the court shall take precautions to guard against the compromise of any CVI, including--
        (A) Permitting the United States to provide the court, ex parte, with a proffer of the witness's response to the question or line of inquiry; and
        (B) Requiring the defendant to provide the court with a proffer of the nature of the information that the defendant seeks to elicit.
    (iii) Obligation of defendant--In any judicial enforcement proceeding, it shall be the defendant's obligation to establish the relevance and materiality of any CVI sought to be introduced.

(8) Construction. Nothing in this subsection shall prevent the United States from seeking protective orders or asserting privileges ordinarily available to the United States to protect

against the disclosure of classified information, including the invocation of the military and State secrets privilege.

(j) Consequences of Violation. Violation of this section is grounds for a civil penalty and other enforcement or corrective action by the Department, and appropriate personnel actions for Federal employees. Corrective action may include issuance of an order requiring retrieval of CVI to remedy unauthorized disclosure or an order to cease future unauthorized disclosure.

(k) Destruction of CVI.

(1) The Department of Homeland Security. Subject to the requirements of the Federal Records Act (5 U.S.C. 105), including the duty to preserve records containing documentation of a Federal agency's policies, decisions, and essential transactions, the Department destroys CVI when no longer needed to carry out the agency's function.

(2) Other covered persons--

(i) In general. A covered person must destroy CVI completely to preclude recognition or reconstruction of the information when the covered person no longer needs the CVI to carry out security measures under paragraph (e) of this section.

(ii) Exception. Section 27.400(k)(2) does not require a State or local government agency to destroy information that the agency is required to preserve under State or local law.

Sec. 27.405 Review and preemption of State laws and regulations.

(a) As per current law, no law, regulation, or administrative action of a State or political subdivision thereof, or any decision or order rendered by a court under state law, shall have any effect if such law, regulation, or decision conflicts with, hinders, poses an obstacle to or frustrates the purposes of this regulation or of any approval, disapproval or order issued there under.

(1) Nothing in this part is intended to displace other federal

requirements administered by the Environmental Protection Agency, U.S. Department of Justice, U.S. Department of Labor, U.S. Department of Transportation, or other federal agencies.

(2) [Reserved]

(b) State law, regulation or administrative action defined. For purposes of this section, the phrase ``State law, regulation or administrative action" means any enacted law, promulgated regulation, ordinance, administrative action, order or decision, or common law standard of a State or any of its political subdivisions.

(c) Submission for review. Any chemical facility covered by these regulations and any State may petition the Department by submitting a copy of a State law, regulation, or administrative action, or decision or order of a court for review under this section.

(d) Review and opinion--

(1) Review. The Department may review State laws, administrative actions, or opinions or orders of a court under State law and regulations submitted under this section, and may offer an opinion whether the application or enforcement of the State law or regulation would conflict with, hinder, pose an obstacle to or frustrate the purposes of this Part.

(2) Opinion. The Department may issue a written opinion on any question regarding preemption. If the question was submitted under subsection (c) of this part, the Assistant Secretary will notify the affected chemical facility and the Attorney General of the subject State of any opinion under this section.

(3) Consultation with States. In conducting a review under this section, the Department will seek the views of the State or local jurisdiction whose laws may be affected by the Department's review.

Sec. 27.410 Third party actions.

(a) Nothing in this Part shall confer upon any person except the

Secretary a right of action, in law or equity, for any remedy including, but not limited to, injunctions or damages to enforce any provision of this Part.

(b) An owner or operator of a chemical facility may petition the Assistant Secretary to provide the Department's view in any litigation involving any issues or matters regarding this Part.

Dated: April 2, 2007.
Michael Chertoff,
Secretary of Homeland Security, Department of Homeland Security.
[FR Doc. E7-6363 Filed 4-6-07; 8:45 am]

BILLING CODE 4410-10-P

Appendix

C

Bibliography

Works Cited

Department of Homeland Security. "Chemical Facility Anti-Terrorism Standards; Final Rule." 6 CFR Part 27. Federal Register. April 9, 2007.

United States Department of Homeland Security. Accessing the Chemical Security Assessment Tool (CSAT) Webpage. http://www.dhs.gov/xprevprot/programs/gc_116950330292 4.shtm. Accessed 27 July 2007.

American Society of Mechanical Engineers, Innovative Technologies Institute,LLC. RAMCAP™. ASME-ITI,LLC. 2005.

Maher, Steven T, and R. Scott Adams, Kennith M. Hall, Carolin M. Keith, Mary F. McDaniel, Stephen R. Melvin. Practical Guide to Risk Management Communications. Mission Viejo: RMP, Inc. 1999.

Department of Homeland Security. "Chemical Facility Anti-Terrorism Standards; Proposed Rule." 6 CFR Part 27. Federal Register. December 28, 2006.

Department of the Army. Field Manual 34-36: <u>Special Operations Forces Intelligence and Electronic Warfare Operations</u>. Appendix D: Target Analysis. 30 September 1991

United States Department of Defense. <u>Department of Defense Dictionary of Military and Associated Terms</u>. Joint Publication 1-02. 12 April 2001. (As Amended Through 13 June 2007.)

Wikipedia. "Computer virus." Webpage. http://en.wikipedia.org/wiki/Computer_virus. Accessed 18 August 2007.

United States Army Fact File: Stryker. Webpage. http://www.army.mil/factfiles/equipment/wheeled/stryker.html. Accessed 18 August 2007.

<u>Vulnerability Assessment Methodology for Chemical Facilities</u> (VAM-CF^{SM}) USDOJ, 2002

<u>Security Vulnerability Assessment Methodology for the Petroleum and Petrochemical Industries, Second Edition</u> October, 2004

<u>Guidelines for Analyzing and Managing the Security Vulnerabilities of Fixed Chemical Sites</u> AIChE, 2003.

United States Department of Homeland Security. "Identifying Facilities Covered by the Chemical Security Regulation Webpage." http://www.dhs.gov/xprevprot/programs/gc_118176584651.shtm. Accessed 18 August 2007.

Security Systems and Technology Center. Systems Analysis and Development Department. "Risk Assessment Methodology for Water (RAM-W^{SM})." Developed in conjunction with

the American Water Works Association. May 2002.

Other Works Of Interest

Newman, Oscar. Creating Defensible Space. United States
   Department of Housing and Urban Development. Office of
   Policy Development and Research. April, 1996.

Appendix

D

Author's Biographies

Stephen R. Melvin, PE CSP CPP, is the President of SRM Associates, Inc. He is an internationally recognized expert in the field of Risk and Safety and has been developing Risk Management and Process Safety Programs for over 15 years. Mr. Melvin provided technical input to the development of several RMP/CalARP guidance documents throughout California and led a diverse team of over 10 people in reviewing, analyzing and making security enhancement recommendations for

over 20 water systems with a combined population of over 1.5 million residents living in California. Mr. Melvin pioneered the implementation of Sandia National Labs Risk Assessment Methodology for Water Utilities (RAM-W^{SM}) for water agency Vulnerability Assessment throughout the state and implemented requirements for compliance with USEPA grant stipulations. He is the author of <u>Keeping Our Neighborhoods Safe</u> which is the only book designed to make anti-terrorism accessible to everyone and which puts anti-terrorism concepts into everyday language. Mr. Melvin is the developer of the "Melvin Method" of antiterrorism, which includes both the "virus theory" of terrorism and a practical approach to bond relationship targeting. He is active in California's Local Emergency Planning Committees (Regions I and VI). He is an active member of the Orange County Private Sector Response

Group and is a member of the Los Angeles Chapter of the FBI's Infragard Program. He is a Navy Reserve Officer and is currently the Officer In Charge for the USS Curts (FFG-38) Reserve Component. He can be reached at: stephen.melvin@oursafetowns.com.

Mr. William R. Benson has over 15 years of security, safety and risk assessment experience in the military and water, petroleum, and chemical industries. Mr. Benson has been involved in a number of Safety Assessments. He has co-authored several technical papers, including "The Impacts of a Major Disaster on Small Local Communities and Some Possible Solutions" and is the author of a 1998 white paper addressing the use of industrial risk methodologies to mitigate the effects of terrorist attacks in critical infrastructures, to include the use of hijacked aircraft used human-guided missiles. The best data miner in the business, his unparalleled skills were essential in developing over 20 risk and safety studies as part of the Risk Management and Process Safety Program overhauls at the TOSCO Los Angeles refineries, experiences instrumental in bringing his military counter-terrorism awareness skills to civilian industries. He participated in numerous Y2K compliance projects, a major North American gold mine, and a nuclear power generating plant. He is CERT trained and served for 2 years as an essential member of the City of Corona's CERT team. He currently serves as a member of the Rockford, Washington Emergency Planning Commission, and is assisting in updating Rockford's Emergency Response Plan to include mitigating the impact of natural or man-made disasters. Mr. Benson was a Counter-Terrorism Instructor for the United States Marine Corps, and is currently serving in the Washington State National Guard as the commander of a Bradley Infantry Fighting Vehicle.

www.ingramcontent.com/pod-product-compliance
Lightning Source LLC
Chambersburg PA
CBHW060623290526
45793CB00001B/122